FORGIVING WHAT THE WORLD
SAYS YOU SHOULDN'T

"In *Forgiving What the World Says You Shouldn't*, Kallista courageously shares her heart-wrenching struggle with generational curses and the power of Christ to break their grip. This raw, authentic journey unveils a forgiveness the world deems impossible. With wisdom and grace, Kallista shows you how to embrace an abundant life and marriage, even in the midst of despair, pain, and fear."

—JULIE REBBOAH,
Founder, From Bud to Bloom Ministry, LLC

"Through sharing her journey, Kallista brings insight into godly principles that can be applied to any relationship. Even when two believers marry, differences will arise, and there will be areas where they are unequally yoked. Even without adultery, there will be wounds, betrayals, and sexual challenges to overcome. Every relationship is an opportunity to extend grace, choose love, and grow in faith. Kallista's book is a courageous testament to love, forgiveness, humility, and resilience."

—RACHAEL HARTMAN,
author of *Called to Write, Chosen to Publish: 20 Inspirational Thoughts for Christian Writers*

"*Forgiving What the World Says You Shouldn't* is a powerful read for couples navigating the complexities of betrayal and forgiveness. Kallista Cazares shares her very personal journey with transparency and vulnerability, offering practical steps to move beyond the pain into healing and restoration. This book is a reminder that God can work with even the most complex of circumstances to facilitate reconciliation when there is love and a heart for forgiveness. This book is a must-read for any couple seeking to rebuild trust and find deeper connection."

—STEVE MCDONALD,
Founder, Walking In Step With God Ministries

"Kallista Cazares tackles a complex and rarely discussed subject with grace, authenticity, and a deep love that flows from her relationship with Christ. This practical and engaging book was developed from Kallista's years of struggle to truly understand love and forgiveness. Her struggles will give you deep insight into those topics, too."

—NELSON SEARCY,
author of *The New You: A Guide to Better Physical, Mental, Emotional, and Spiritual Wellness*

Forgiving What the World Says You Shouldn't

*Releasing the Chains of Bitterness
in Unequally Yoked Marriages*

KALLISTA CAZARES

Foreword by Sam Serio

RESOURCE *Publications* • Eugene, Oregon

FORGIVING WHAT THE WORLD SAYS YOU SHOULDN'T
Releasing the Chains of Bitterness in Unequally Yoked Marriages

Copyright © 2025 Kallista Cazares. All rights reserved. Except for brief quotations in critical publications or reviews, no part of this book may be reproduced in any manner without prior written permission from the publisher. Write: Permissions, Wipf and Stock Publishers, 199 W. 8th Ave., Suite 3, Eugene, OR 97401.

Resource Publications
An Imprint of Wipf and Stock Publishers
199 W. 8th Ave., Suite 3
Eugene, OR 97401

www.wipfandstock.com

PAPERBACK ISBN: 979-8-3852-2495-1
HARDCOVER ISBN: 979-8-3852-2496-8
EBOOK ISBN: 979-8-3852-2497-5

04/01/25

*To my husband, Corey,
Thank you for your humility and support
in writing this book.
Without you, there would be empty pages.
I love you.*

"So we fix our eyes not on what is seen, but on what is unseen. For what is seen is temporary, but what is unseen is eternal."

(2 Corinthians 4:18)

Contents

Foreword by Sam Serio | ix

Author's Note | xi

Introduction | xiii

CHAPTER ONE
In the Secret Place | 3

CHAPTER TWO
Drawing Near to God | 17

CHAPTER THREE
Recommitting to Values | 30

CHAPTER FOUR
Rejecting the Devil's Lies | 44

CHAPTER FIVE
Forgiving Daily | 59

CHAPTER SIX
Vulnerability | 71

CHAPTER SEVEN
Restoring Trust | 81

CHAPTER EIGHT
Rekindling Romance | 89

CHAPTER NINE
Letting Love in Again | 104

CHAPTER TEN
Allowing Yourself to Be Transformed | 118

About the Author | 133

Bibliography | 135

Foreword

Forgiving What the World Says You Shouldn't is intensely practical and deeply personal. All of us have people in our lives who have disappointed, betrayed, mistreated, or hurt us. This book specifically shows you how to forgive sexual betrayal. Kallista will take you on a journey you will not forget. It is written both from weakness and strength, pain and grace. She has been there and done that and now teaches you how to forgive your spouse. She covers everything from A to Z, leaving out nothing—you will be transformed just like she was.

God comforts us so that we can show others that same comfort we received from Him (2 Cor 1:3-4). That is exactly what happens here. You will be amazed at her story and her triumph; no pity party here. She writes from her heart and from God's heart, shown in the Bible. I loved all the verses she uses to carefully explain what happened in the past and what will happen in the future because she has hidden His Word in her memory.

It is evident she has done the hard work in learning how to truly and permanently forgive. Adultery is a life changer where all your dreams for the future have now been demolished and devastated. When others would throw in the towel, she rolls up her sleeves and shows you how to do the same! I hope you enjoy this book, as much as I have. I have seen the pain and heartache in spouses who were betrayed. I have heard the cries of husbands and wives who are unequally yoked together and how frustrating it is for each of them. Kallista helps you navigate these extreme stormy waters wisely.

She gets the bigger picture of life—our holiness is more important to Him than our fleeting emotions. She truly wants to become more like Jesus and knows that He uses tough times to conform us to His image and likeness. Holiness brings that joy—and she teaches you how to experience an inner joy and peace that the world does not give. Her advice is something the world does not understand, so beware.

This book just might change your life and your situation more than you can ever imagine. But then, isn't that what God does—He can do more than you could comprehend in giving you a strength that you never knew possible. Healing sexual and emotional hurt is not beyond His abilities. After all, Jesus came to set the captives free and it is so easy to be a prisoner to bitterness and rage today.

Kallista shows you that love and forgiveness is the better way to live. It won't be easy at first but then you will experience a closeness to God you never dreamed possible as you rely on His powerful Word each day. You won't forget this book—even if you want to—when people that you have loved and trusted hurt you to your very core, and they will.

Heaven is the only place with no pain, and this book teaches you how to experience that Heaven on Earth. It shows you how the Word and presence of the Lord help you run and not be weary. Thank you, Kallista, for showing us your trauma and your triumph. Thank you for teaching us how to do the same in whatever difficulty and disappointment He allows to come into our lives!

Pastor, Author, and Dr. Sam Serio
President and Founder of Healing Sexual Hurt
www.HealingSexualHurt.com

Author's Note

As I write about the most private parts of my marriage, I can't help but ponder that no marriage is alike. Every couple who is unequally yoked has their own story. Most often, these situations occur when a relationship is built upon sin. For others, maybe they ended up there unexpectedly when a spouse backslid. Regardless, I'm confident the Lord will use testimonies like ours to reach others around us who struggle silently and are in desperate need of encouragement.

I am convinced the Word of God has been given to us to bring hope, comfort, and peace in moments like these when all else around us feels impossible. However, this relates to you; thank you for picking up this book. I hope these pages lift your spirit amid your journey and that you not only survive your marriage but also learn to thrive as a Christian and with your spouse despite spiritual differences.

This book is not a ten-step program; it is about forgiveness, seeking God's will, obeying and applying Scripture, and allowing Him to transform your life and marriage.

Please know I am not testing to take on the role of a woman pastor. I am simply a born again Christian, wife, and mother who has experienced what you are going through. By God's grace, my relationship is recovering from the affair and beginning to thrive. Fortunately, I have found hope in Jesus Christ and am now reaping the fruits of choosing to stay saved and married—which I hope to share with others who choose to remain married and seek healing.

For couples with unique circumstances, I do not condone anyone staying married while being abused and understand that, at times, there are no other options but to separate when it puts people's lives at risk or if your spouse is unwilling to change.

I strongly believe in creating healthy boundaries and protecting yourself and your children. I do not know it all or want to act like I have it all together. My reason for writing this book is that God has placed it on my heart to share pieces of my testimony so that others encountering infidelity in their marriage can find hope, be set free from bitterness, and stay committed to the Lord while remaining committed to their unsaved spouse. There is beauty after the storm.

Introduction

His white 2011 Chevrolet Tahoe was turning right, and I was supposed to go left. Instead, I contemplated and then turned right. He didn't see me because he drove fast, but I couldn't miss him with his lifted truck ahead of me. I followed him to his apartment because my flesh couldn't resist the temptation of spending alone time with him. For half a year, we kept our distance from one another and adhered to the necessary boundaries, as my church headship and parents cautiously advised. Their efforts worked to protect us for a while until I didn't want them to work anymore.

You see, we all have free will to pray daily, stay accountable, and feed our spirit—but when you choose to do the opposite, you place yourself in dangerous territory. Which took me to a place I never thought I would go. Since I had already backslidden two times before, I was all too familiar with testing the limits. This time, I would go too far.

I ignored all the red flags trying to deter me in the opposite direction. I also ignored that it was spiritually fatal and detrimental to my faith. My father warned me. My friends warned me. My headship called me directly, advising against jumping into marriage straight out from fornicating and encouraging me to repent. I knew better. Every sermon I had heard taught me better. God's Word taught me better.

Sin will take you to a place where you feel like there is no way out but *your* way. And oh, I would soon discover feelings are fleeting. When we are stubborn and hard-headed, the plans we make for ourselves will never be better than the plans God wants to bless us with.

Three months after living together, I became pregnant. The decision was made in the heat of the moment, and I was glad to become a mother. However, I was doing the one thing I told myself I would never do: I was having a child out of wedlock.

I knew that my child would carry the weight of my sin. Unfortunately, one day, our decision will have lofty consequences that will inevitably try to grip our firstborn and hold her back from serving God. This is why I pray fervently, with tears, pleading with God to set her life apart despite our mistakes. Ultimately, we can only contend and have faith in Jesus that she might be spared from the generational curses that were too heavy for us to bear.

Two months after that was October. On the twenty-fourth, we decided to marry. When we made this decision, we knew we were not ready. Not mentally, not spiritually, not financially, but we did it anyway. The days leading up to our marriage and the days after were filled with heart-wrenching arguments, anger, and regret. I knew the only way we could sustain a marriage founded on fornication would be to repent and keep Jesus centered in our lives. To have Him as our firm foundation would spiritually equip us with the right mindset we needed to remain faithful to one another.

Moving forward, more mistakes were made. One could say our recurring arguments were due to selfishness, which they absolutely were. However, above all other things, they were exclusively derived from being unequally yoked. And like the stubborn young woman I was, I tried with all my might to steer my husband to repentance—something only the Holy Spirit can do—instead of being a crown to his head.

That is because my former spirit of contentiousness only pushed him farther away from Jesus and me. And believe me, feeling a million miles away from your spouse while you both sleep next to each other in bed is the last thing any married man or woman wants. There are two ways the battle can be fought:

INTRODUCTION

spiritually or carnally. The reality is we have a natural aggression that rises—our flesh—that wants to take control of a situation when something doesn't work in our favor. But the best way to channel your energy in times like these is to pray. Pray over your husband's head while he sleeps. Pray for him while you lay hands on the areas of your home where he sits or lays most often. Nothing else will work as well as this. We only wish we would have heeded wise counsel sooner.

Part 1

CHAPTER ONE

In the Secret Place

It was a Sunday. Not different from most because fighting about going to church together was normal in our marriage. Quite honestly, with the way things were headed for us, my desire to attend church, be in the presence of God with like-minded believers, and receive healing and direction grew stronger each day. So I couldn't understand why Corey and I struggled to agree on the matter since we shared similar views before saying, "I do." Both our families had raised us in church. I grew up in church at The Door, and Corey's mom introduced him to our sister church, The Potter's House, years prior. Nonetheless, despite the normalcy of our arguing over that matter, something different was brewing that evening.

Finally, we headed to church for a revival service (four days of preaching by a guest pastor or evangelist) and got fed a great word about how secret sin gets in the way between you and salvation, which stirred both of our hearts. Then, by the end of the service, my husband surprisingly responded to the altar call while the piano played a gentle tune in the background and walked to the front steps for prayer.

After months of backsliding and leaving the church, I noticed my husband's heart grew hardened toward God and righteous things. So I was happy when Corey knelt down on the old, familiar church carpet for repentance. Truly, the softening of his heart and responsiveness toward the Holy Spirit was an answered prayer—a prayer that felt like I had been waiting on for a lifetime but was only the first fourteen months of our marriage.

While I was joyful God was moving upon his heart, Corey was still waging a silent battle within himself that followed us home that evening. I didn't know what was coming next—pain, the pain was next.

After service, we got home and began arguing again. He was grumbling about me being unhappy, filled with regret for fornicating, having a child out of wedlock, and rushing into marriage with a man who "wasn't the Christian man I wanted." I cried. I was so tired. To some extent, he was right—I often felt self-condemnation regarding backsliding for the third time and our impulsive decision to marry quickly. I wondered when the random fights would come to an end. The master bedroom we stayed in at my grandparent's house was filled with a spirit of division and contentiousness. As a child who grew accustomed to seeing married couples fight, it was challenging trying to navigate ourselves out of it; I am sure my husband can attest to this also.

Although the master bedroom was the biggest room in the house, it typically felt stuffy and restrictive, adding to our feelings of frustration. It helped that the walls were white, and the carpet was pulled out and replaced with laminate flooring, though it still wasn't enough. There had been many times our fights would escalate, causing me to feel unsafe and emotionally unstable in our tiny house of a room. Unfortunately, we were both native to occupying a room where our problems imploded the four walls of our living space.

Often, after an argument with each other, his hurtful words would resonate with me and cause me to sink into myself. As we lay beside one another, I accepted the feelings roaring through my head and tried to forgive him before falling asleep, but I was drifting quickly with our eight-month-old daughter at my side. Until the tense silence was broken with a confession I had been yearning and suspicious of for months.

"Kallista . . . I lied. I cheated."

After hearing the words, I couldn't believe it. It's like my mind put up this wall to protect itself from the verbal attacks it received time and time again. Still half asleep, I asked him, "What?" my mind was rejecting the words, and they weren't registering. He repeated himself. Again, in confusion, I questioned out loud, "You lied? You cheated?" he confirmed. My heart started to race, and tears streaming down my face as I lay motionless. My husband apologized and told me he would understand if I never forgave him. I asked, "How long ago? How many times?" he said, "A year ago and once."

For a year, I had battled insecurity and lack of trust after finding texts and images exchanged between him and other women on his phone. After each discovery, I would repeat the process of doing my best to trust him and stop living in constant fear. I loved him and desperately wanted the marriage to work. Our relationship, my family, and my sanity were at stake. It wasn't until I finally gave my worries to the Lord and begged Him to bring anything that was hidden into the light. Doing so helped me find peace of mind in those months of waiting. It was a matter of God showing me the truth about *His* timing. I knew He would bring complete exposure when He thought would be fit—now was that time.

Quickly, my sadness morphed into anger. I sat on the edge of the bed beside him and began cursing at him, pushing him, hitting him, and telling him I hated him. Deep down, I felt hatred for her, someone I had never met. Although I wondered if she was the one I had found on his phone multiple times before, he confessed it was. Corey began to caress me while he cried, repeatedly apologizing for all the damage that was done. He was so remorseful, repentant, and honest that night; how could I not accept his apology? As badly as I wanted to be held, I didn't want to forgive him, nor did I want his love right then and there.

I reckon that is why 2 Corinthians 6:14 warns followers of Christ not to be entangled with unbelievers. While Paul may not have primarily spoken on marriage for this verse, it certainly is fitting. That is because God wants us to understand one thing clearly through this message: being unequally yoked with unbelievers binds us to the decisions and actions of others who hold other moral standards that do not align with Jesus's values and purposes.

Though, deep, deep down inside, I was relieved. I desperately wanted Corey to act like himself again and thought that maybe by releasing this secret, he would be free to do that. I missed having conversations in the car together that would last for hours. I missed his affection and sensitivity. I missed that gleam in his brown hazel eyes that led me down the path to his mind. I always loved to pick his brain about his upbringing—what life had been like without a father, the conflict he faced growing up, what was important to him, and his plans for the future. I always admired that he was driven and resilient despite his past. I admired his imperfections because he loved me even after knowing my life's darkest and ugliest secrets. I had faith that, through Corey's confession, he would come back to me, and we could have a real chance at reconciliation.

Finally, after all the messages I found of him smooth-talking other women, all the graphics in his phone that I allowed to stain my mind, all the passive-aggressiveness would soon come to an end. The heart issue was finally being addressed, and for that, I was grateful. It was bittersweet that God's promise had come to pass, "For nothing is hidden that will not be made manifest, nor is anything secret that will not be known and come to light" (Luke 8:17). A blessing in disguise because once the secrets had been exposed, we were confronted with the need for change. The options were: To stay or to go. Change or not change? Heal or not heal?

It was like a tragic Shakespeare moment where you decide whether to be or not to be. The truth is, I did not want to be. I did not want to be alive because staying on earth meant having to battle with this new reality. I did not want to be his wife because it meant having to reap the consequences of fornicating and rushing into a lifetime commitment with him. I did not want to—amid all the chaos, I was reminded I am a mother, and to entertain the idea of ending my life was selfish. What would become of my daughter if I decided to leave so swiftly? What would become of her future, her children's future, and her grandchildren's future?

FAMILY HISTORY

I was raised by my mother and my maternal side of the family in South Texas. My mom and dad never married so I spent almost every other weekend with my father's side of the family growing up. Although growing up in a broken home, some of my happiest memories come from spending time with relatives from each side. Thankfully, as I entered adulthood, I was blessed with the opportunity to begin creating happy memories with my parents, too.

Before we got there though, my mom worked full-time while she went to college to become a nurse and provided for my little brother and me as a single mother. We lived with my grandparents for some years, which is why I grew up so closely with my maternal grandparents. I spent a lot of my time singing oldies, writing covers of songs, playing outside, and walking the streets with my friends. I felt safe in my home and enjoyed being primarily raised by my maternal family, although it was difficult to build a closer relationship with my mom for years because she was emotionally unavailable then.

As for my dad, our relationship was touch and go for a while when he was battling depression after the death of his first wife. I grew up noticing he was well respected in his neighborhood and always looked out for other people. He would wave at strangers and shelter me as much as possible from hearing and watching secular things. Even though he wasn't always emotionally and physically present, I admired his efforts to protect me and spend quality time together even with everything that was going on in his private life.

Ultimately, the relationship I had with my parents were distant and strained. I carried many burdens with me as a result of their mental and spiritual struggles, absence, and poor choices. Despite their flaws, I knew they loved me and I held on to that tightly. What I didn't know yet was how their misfortunes and dysfunctional patterns could later impact me—as you will read soon.

Let's just say I am blessed that God has restored both relationships with my parents. I am grateful for the bond I have with my mom today and for her acknowledging past mistakes. She has been a loving mother I can depend on and always shows up when I need her. I am also grateful that my dad became a born-again Christian and has been saved for well over twelve years—set free from rage, drug addiction, and suicide. By God's grace, my dad is one of the first in our family to walk in truth genuinely. I am confident that his decisions to repent and find healing through Jesus have positively and indirectly affected my life and personal struggles.

UNDER THE CURSE

As I grew older, I began to get nosey and question why my parents didn't work out. The situation is complex, and since this isn't their story, I will not pretend to know what happened. Though, I am sure unfaithfulness, drug abuse, and other issues were involved. Later, it was no surprise that before their relationship, unfaithfulness was already a curse to previous relatives.

These sins and the spirit of division have been deeply embedded in my maternal side of the family for five generations. For all I know, it can also be a curse that runs through my paternal side. While talking with my aunt about this book, she shared something insightful with me. She told me that infidelity could be traced as far back as my great-great-great-grandmother and grandfather. However, I suspect the curse of adultery goes back even further than our knowledge.

My great-grandmother Antonia told the story of how her grandmother Guadalupe encountered spiritual attacks from adulteress women when living in Mexico. At the time, one or two women took on the form of a shapeshifting owl, also known as the lechuza. According to her, she would sometimes hear the lechuza walking and making loud sounds from the top of her home, scratching its claws, and that it shifted into the face of the two women whom her husband had an affair with.

In an effort to protect herself, she would begin cursing the shapeshifter (saying a spell) while tying knots on a rope until the witch (adulteress woman) fell off the roof and disappeared. Insane right? Although I discovered an unexpected truth about my relatives' involvement in witchcraft, I also gained perspective. I could clearly see all these curses at work in my life that had been passed down from generation to generation. *Who would break the cycle of infidelity?*

In addition to my generational curses, my husband also had his own that he was dealing with. Growing up, Corey learned some problematic things about his birth story, which involved him being born from adultery. Before getting married, Corey and I knew that adultery was a potential curse for both of us, all things considered. Aside from his personal feelings regarding his father's choices, he expressed that he didn't want to follow in the same footsteps.

The generational curses of infidelity threatened us both, and the Devil assaulted our minds in those early months of marriage, almost causing me to fall and ensnare him. However, with time, the prime difference between us became salvation. As you know, without salvation, we are prisoners of sin. That is why I am confident Corey's initial intention was to love me, and his wedding vows were genuine. Until, his efforts to overcome sin without God failed him.

> "The Lord, the Lord God, merciful and gracious, longsuffering, and abounding in goodness and truth, keeping mercy for thousands, forgiving iniquity and transgression and sin, by no means clearing the guilty, visiting the iniquity of the fathers upon the children and the children's children to the third and the fourth generation." (Exod. 34:6-7)

Though we knew rushing into marriage without righting our wrongs (repenting and fleeing fornication) would be a great challenge, we were blinded by sin and had no real clue what monster we were up against—generations of unprecedented adultery far beyond our understanding. Overcoming sin and generational curses requires total surrendering and dependency on Jesus Christ.

As soon as God showed me this, I began to connect the dots of other generational curses: physical abuse, emotional abuse, verbal abuse, division, drug abuse, and suicide and refused to fold under the Devil's trickiest devices. I had seen the damage these reversals brought upon couples and their children my whole life as I looked toward my father, cousin, and other relatives. So, I chose life.

Quite literally, I chose to live, fight, and contend for my marriage. I chose these things because I had already witnessed the repercussions of divorce and separation of those who threw in the towel prematurely without asking God what He wanted for their life; such a decision is selfish and detrimental in all its facets.

From my experiences, and those of others, divorce is like cancer; it wraps itself around divorcees so tightly that the growing hatred they have for their ex strangles all joy from their lives. I've witnessed it destroy the hope of children who no longer believe in love or marriage and are robbed of experiencing God's true intent for family.

That is when I knew I had to handle these violations differently. The ugly reality was my husband, and I had fornicated and *chose* to leave the church. Three years later, I understood that my unresolved feelings toward my father and depression over the loss of a boyfriend had me yearning to fill a void only Jesus could fill. I found fleeting comfort in Corey's admiration and determination to make me feel special the way I longed for from my dad and felt robbed of happiness by the sudden death of Eden (EJ). These issues festered in my soul like an infected wound. Again, my unresolved issues and a lack of maintaining my heart made the door to sin accessible to me.

I acknowledge that neither of our hearts was right with the Lord, and it was only a matter of time before we would reap what we sowed. Slowly, my anger started shifting from him and her to our sin. It became clear to me again why our congregation tried so hard to deter us from fornicating and marrying quickly—to avoid this heartache and trail of tears.

A paradigm shift took place within me. How could I express all of my anger toward my husband and this other woman when they did not know Christ themselves? Didn't my favorite scripture urge me for years to "Forgive them, for they know not what they do" (Luke 23:34)? I continuously looked back on how this all started to observe from a bird's-eye view.

We had known about each other since we were children: Corey was a boyfriend of mine in second grade, though he claims not to remember. While remembering that he dumped me in the lunch line for farting on our way to recess was slightly annoying, it also revived the dry humor inside me that was desperately needed. Thinking about our history and observing his face during car rides gently tugged me toward recalling all the goofy, childish moments we shared.

I grew convicted by the Holy Spirit that it was my appointed time to stop bathing in this tub of hatred, anger, depression, self-righteousness, insecurity, self-harm, and entitlement. Spewing curses at my spouse and physically attacking him caused more damage, which would later require extensive care and healing in other areas. Not only was holding Corey's mistake against him constantly destructive for him, but it was taking a toll on my emotional health, physical health, and salvation. As much as I tried to combat the fiery darts of the Devil, I couldn't dodge feelings of unworthiness and unforgiveness, both of which drove a thick wedge between God and me.

Not only was reacting vulgarly unhealthy, but it was profitless. I gained nothing from despising, belittling, and making Corey inferior to me. No matter what I could say or do, it wouldn't have changed the pain I was feeling. Thankfully, I found direction and encouragement by turning to the word.

> "Cease from anger, and forsake wrath; Do not fret—it only causes harm. For evildoers shall be cut off; But those who wait on the Lord, They shall inherit the earth." (Ps. 37:8-9)

Finally, my unending resentment toward Corey was physically draining because I was always tired from unending stress and crying. I would cry in bed, in the shower, in the garage, at church, in the car, and while eating at our favorite restaurant. Every time I would talk to him, I wanted to bring up the conversation again and repeatedly ask him why. Choosing anger and stagnancy made me tired. I was exhausted from the thoughts and from crying. I would constantly self-sabotage because I couldn't stop thinking about it. Bitterness was cutting circulation off my lifeline to God, peace, and joy—I had to break free from the curse that stood before us.

Personally, it was hard to get the affair out of my head, like any unresolved trauma. When I would cease progress or take a step in the opposite direction of forgiving my husband, I was inflicting unnecessary pain on myself. Truth be told, I felt like I deserved it, a sorry lie from Hell. All my life, I have been used to being a victim. When my dad wasn't around growing up, I was a victim. When I got molested as a child, I was a victim. When I was raped, I was a victim. When my boyfriend died, I was a victim. And when my husband cheated on me, I was a victim again.

While by definition, I am defined as a victim in these cases, I didn't have to submit myself to self-pity. By refusing to "cease from anger" and fretting over the situation, I opened the door to self-destruction. The Devil was whispering lies about my self-worth to kill me, and I let it go as far as punching myself in the face, slapping myself, and choking myself behind closed doors. I felt self-destruction and saw it bruising me everywhere.

While you grow in hatred for your husband, you will consequently increase in distance from God. Putting your salvation on the line is a dark road you don't want to go on. So draw near to the One who loves you more than anybody else. Take refuge in His peace and beware of the Devil, who will make you question your decision to stay. Who will whisper sweet lies and groom your fragile emotions by making it seem as if you are compromising your dignity?

The Devil doesn't want you to forgive; he wants you to rot in bitterness. Therefore, do the opposite. Because what comes so naturally to us as humans is spiritually detrimental and will damage us to the core. Fight through prayer, asking God to show you how to forgive what seems unforgivable.

GOD CAN USE WHAT WAS INTENDED FOR EVIL FOR GOOD

This journey has the potential to make or break your marriage. More specifically, it has the potential to make or break you. Will you choose spiritual life or spiritual death? Because God wants so desperately to save, redeem, restore, and liberate you and transform your marriage, but do you share His same values? Are you lost in the eye of the storm?

My former pastor Richard Rubi once said, "Love is not a feeling; it is a choice." I find this concept immensely profound, especially in my unequally yoked marriage. Since my husband and I share differences one can only imagine how often disagreements arise. Though disagreements occurred frequently in our early years of marriage, we are learning that our different stances on particular matters do not have to mean our marriage is a dud. In cases where my spouse does something I disagree with or speaks a certain way, I choose to love him regardless of his actions.

Likewise, when I sometimes overstep my boundaries in pushing my beliefs onto him, he sees past those moments by reminding me he understands and respects what I believe but kindly asks me not to make him do things he's not ready to commit himself to yet. Furthermore, just as much as I choose to love my husband despite his affair, he also chooses to love me despite my mistakes. (Yes, even as a Christian wife and mother, I have had my fair share of wrongdoings.)

For instance, at times when I have fallen short of God's glory at the beginning of our marriage and returned to pornography or have allowed curiosities of old soul ties to manifest and result in me looking them up to see where they are in life, Corey has chosen to forgive me and move forward. We share expectations that our future actions will demonstrate genuine remorse through tangible change. All of these are perfect examples of how we choose to love each other despite the feelings we have regarding that person's sin. While not advocating for unequally yoked marriages to accept repeated offenses, I am saying that through genuine remorse and change in one's actions, it is possible to reconcile with your spouse and come out stronger for it in the end.

When you said "I do," you promised, for better or worse, through (spiritual) sickness and health. Your spouse needs you to forgive. Your children need you to forgive. You need to forgive. And ultimately, God calls you to forgiveness.

A part of becoming more Christ-like looks like laying everything down at the feet of Jesus and forgiving others like He has forgiven you (Eph. 4:32). And I know that everything I am saying goes against the grain in our 21st-century culture. Where feminism and self-love prevail above all good things on earth, please remember God reigns above it all.[1] At a crossroads like this, it is pivotal to establish yourself in Christ's firm foundation—doing so brings forth blessing. If I had retaliated or made the decision to leave my husband before trying to make things work, I would never have witnessed the change that happened inside of him. After confessing to committing adultery, he stopped talking to other women cold turkey. While his walk with God was short-lived after this repentance, he has proven honest and trustworthy ever since. Now is a good moment to pause and reflect on whether you already lived for Christ before this tribulation.

If you have strayed away in your walk or have never fully committed to living your life for Jesus, "God says, the 'right time' is now, today is the day of salvation" (2 Cor. 6:2). When you allow God to be at the center of all aspects of your life, especially your marriage, you will discover His hope for you is that, in a godly and biblically aligned marriage, or unequally yoked marriage, divorce would not be an option because of mutual respect and devotion. Allow me to clarify: I'm not suggesting that women remain in unsafe marriages. Instead, I'm coming against our innate urge to run amid being wronged. Since being wronged is closely related to

---

1. Nika Palmer, "Self-Love Is a Feminist Issue," January 23, 2020.

feeling like you are in danger, it is understanding that our fight or flight mode kicks in.

However, we must be careful and intentional in these next steps because they are critical decisions that will determine the future of our families' lives. Friend, I understand you are facing tragedy, violation, and maybe even verbal, emotional, and domestic violence, as I once did. However, more often than not, choosing to end your marriage without attempting to fight for it is not always a sustainable solution.

Experiencing an affair in your marriage is a pain that no one can run from—especially when you share a child with them. Dealing with these things throughout my pregnancy and after the baby was born was one of the hardest things I've ever had to do. Since I didn't have work obligations and had the privilege of staying home with her, I spent my days lying with her, crying often, and praying a lot. Unfortunately, there were moments when I would grow easily frustrated with her crying and yelling out of frustration when I was having a difficult time sleeping at night. Then my husband would have to remind me that my anger was at him and not her. This truth would cause me to reevaluate my actions.

At times like these, I wanted to run away from the pain I felt because now it directly affected our daughter, and I couldn't help but feel like a bad mom and that she would be better off without me. However, I knew my family would not benefit from this decision long-term because my daughter would always be looking up to me, regardless of whether I was there or not. I wanted to set an example of how to overcome the pains of life that my daughter could look up to should she ever, God forbid, find herself in my shoes.

I want Aria to be resilient and understand that my decisions, whether to give in or break these curses, would play a massive role in shaping her into that. It was only by the grace of God and prayers from my family and church friends that I overcame this. With that said, an affair inflicts a deep wound that requires proper treatment to heal correctly—this looks like daily prayer and forgiveness, leaning on headship, and taking actionable steps to mend your marriage, as I mention in later chapters. Otherwise, the wound will become sorely infected and dangerous to your health and family.

Similarly, if not correctly cared for, heart problems of unforgiveness, insecurity, and depression will manifest inside your heart and into your marriage, which germinate into an infected wound, as previously described. Failing to recognize and deal with these red flags can also negatively impact our children since they look up to us and pick up on everything we say and do.

Should you neglect your wounded spirit, it will cripple you in various areas of your life, causing you to struggle later to maintain healthy human relationships or even prevent you from loving yourself. Gently, I remind you that divorce may be necessary for marriages that are physically unsafe or undergo repetitive cheating. This is largely different from choosing divorce out of mere anger and believing the lie that you will never be able to forgive your spouse truly, or "once a cheater, always a cheater." These are lies from Hell that cut corners to purposely avoid having to forgive your spouse and the other woman.

Regardless of your decision to stay or leave, the wound will always require proper maintenance to move forward healthily. As long as you draw near to Christ, He will sustain you, establish His throne in your unequally yoked marriage by sanctifying your unsaved husband through you as a Christian wife (1 Cor. 7:13-14), and instill a sense of peace in your relationship like no other. That is His promise, and this is your inheritance. My prayer is for you to see this book goes against the grain of divorce, is about choosing to *stay*, and provides the spiritual tools that God equips us with in the Bible to be overcomers.

CHAPTER TWO

Drawing Near to God

"Draw near to God and He will draw near to you."
—James 4:8

Have you considered the confession, or finding out about your spouse's affair, is an answered prayer? I understand that it can be challenging under such circumstances to believe this, but if you were praying for truth and God gave it to you, consider your prayers answered. When affairs are brought to light, we should accept them as a fulfillment of God's promise to protect His people.

As mentioned in the last chapter, the Lord promises to those saved to bring what is done in the dark out into the light. Despite the emotional turmoil involved in this discovery, please recognize that this is a blessing in disguise under all of the pain. Discovering this violation and confronting unresolved heart issues head-on opens the door to redemption. Fortunately, the gifts of redemption bring healing and restoration to all lost or stolen from you. So, have you thanked God for keeping His promises?

If your response is yes, that's great! Now, translate that gratefulness into praise during prayer. On another note, if you are struggling to proceed in this area, I encourage you to pray to God. Take your troubling circumstances, unwelcoming emotions, or even any unexpected temptations to Him and fervently seek His wisdom. Take heart, the Lord hears and sees your every struggle. Reach out to Him and be teachable as He works out the transformation in your life.

About a week after discovering, I raised my hand to go to the altar to seek forgiveness for my bitterness and hatred toward my husband and the unwanted invader in our marriage. I was met with a woman in the church. A woman who had experienced what I had and understood the pain I was going through—right in that moment, I was confronted with Christ's stillness and confirmation that "Yes, forgiveness is the will He has for all of our lives."

Shockingly though, the sister looked at me and asked, "Are you truly ready to forgive your husband?" as I stared dumbfounded, it became clear to me that forgiving my spouse was going to require more of me than just going to the altar and getting my heart right with God. It would also demand that I make a decision daily to forgive and rebuke the thoughts of the affair that attack my mind.

I understand now that she was fully aware of the battle that lay ahead for the journey I was beginning. When she asked that question, it did not draw an insulted feeling from my heart, but rather a challenge to fight against the spiritual opposition and internal conflict waging within me.

I quickly learned that replaying the scenario in my head almost every hour every day for weeks was killing me. It created unnecessary tension and a higher wall between my husband and me. This mistake taught me that I should have first taken my pain and agony to Jesus. I should have first poured out my heart to Him instead of inflicting physical pain on my husband and additional damage on myself.

Pouring out my heart to God was the most refreshing thing I could have done in this situation, and I regretted not unloading my burdens to Him first (1 Sam. 1:10, Ps. 62:8). When I drew near to Christ, my mind was transformed from bitterness to forgiveness.

The Lord began outpouring His unfailing love over my life, and His presence was undeniable at many times when I least expected to feel Him.

By immersing myself in Scripture every time I felt depression, anger, and insecurities rising, I was inviting His promises to become real in my life. Even when I didn't *feel* like it, I knew I needed to open up my Bible or YouVersion app. It was like I was being deprived of air, and if I couldn't receive God's breath of life within me to revive my spirit, I was going to die. On the contrary, by neglecting my prayer life and skipping daily reading, I was subjecting myself to long, never-ending, painful days filled with tormenting thoughts.

FORGIVENESS IS GOD'S NATURE

Through fervent prayer and contending, God began to deal with the depths of my heart. As I strived to be more Christ-like, an unexpected conviction grew on me. No matter how hard I tried to resist the Holy Spirit, what the Lord required of me was undeniable. First, after spewing words of hate and cursing over this other woman's life, God dealt with me and not only wanted me to apologize but to ask her to forgive *me* for the things *I* said and thought about her in secret. Secondly, He was challenging me to lead her to Christ.

As I previously mentioned, my favorite scripture has always been, "Forgive them, Father, for they know not what they do." With this scripture in mind, an unrelenting pain grew in my heart until I followed through with what the Lord asked of me. Only by drawing near and crying out to Him was I able to repent of my sins of bitterness and hatred, which supernaturally led me to the feet of Christ. At the end of the day, I knew He wanted me to share the gospel and be an authentic Christ-like example to demonstrate the love of Jesus for her through forgiveness.

> "Do not take revenge, my dear friends, but leave room for God's wrath, for it is written: "It is mine to

avenge; I will repay," says the Lord. On the contrary: "If your enemy is hungry, feed him; if he is thirsty, give him something to drink." (Rom. 12:19-21)

So I prayed continuously for a miracle until He provided the strength to do what my flesh resisted. He gave me the courage to do it all, and when I texted her, this woman wore her heart on her sleeve. After telling her I forgave her and asked for her forgiveness for all of the ill things I had wished upon her life, I then asked if she had ever heard of the name of Jesus and if she knew He had died for her sins.

The conversation continued, and I told her that she would not make Heaven her home if she continued on the path she was walking. She agreed with me and said she wasn't sure if she would make Heaven her home if she died tomorrow. So I sent her a sinner's prayer that she could say and provided a local sister church's address that she could attend if she were serious about her repentance.

By the end of our conversation, my heart felt free. I cried tears of joy because I felt like God had unlocked this new chapter in my journey of healing and restoration. I was finally happy. As a matter of fact, I'm almost crying now because of how grateful I am to have encountered this victory and still be reaping its benefits. Now, I won't pretend that certain thoughts have entirely vanished. They still try to claw their way into my mind, but this time was different. It was different because as I contended to feed my spirit, God provided the willpower and self-control to resist my flesh.

When thoughts tried to pass through the gates, I finally could take dominion by telling them no. Most times, I would have to speak out loud and rebuke the thoughts that were trying to penetrate through my heart to bring me down. I refused by choosing to forgive daily. It wasn't just enough to say I forgave once and allow my emotions to consume me later.

Forgiveness is an act that must be done repeatedly every time that thought resurfaces, whether days, months, or years later.

The lesson I learned was that if it is through prayer that we can obtain peace of mind, it is through edifying ourselves with

Scripture that we can obtain His perspective and walk in His truth. Oppositely, when we become prideful, thinking we can deal with our pain and manage our trials alone, we push God away and separate ourselves from those around us. This is very common to do after you get hurt because you are so focused on yourself, nothing else seems to matter. It's understandable that what you are going through is painful, but it's essential not to forget who is on the throne, no matter your situation.

Placing this barrier between you and God is like restricting blood flow to an artery. We need God all the time, especially when facing such challenges. If you become hardened toward God and refuse to draw near to him, you will develop heart issues. Focusing on the past—mistakes made and hurtful experiences—can make us feel far from Him. If you are battling anger, depression, or anything else, that is a clear sign that your heart has wandered.

Allowing my pride and anger to reign over temporary circumstances before God is something I experienced firsthand. That is how I can tell you it is the last thing you want to do. No matter how upset you are or how right you think you are, nothing can justify putting God last—doing so causes you to be lukewarm.

> "Pride goes before destruction, and a haughty spirit before a fall. Better to be of a humble spirit with the lowly, than to divide the spoil with the proud." (Prov. 16:18-19)

In other words—for the sake of this context—allowing your feelings to run rampant will always lead to spiritual corruption. Here's a story of mine that can help you identify how this plays out negatively in one's life while navigating through marriage after infidelity.

Shortly after I discovered the affair, I allowed my resentment to not only bring division in my marriage through pettiness and contentiousness, but I allowed it to get in between my Savior and me. There were countless times before re-dedicating myself, I was tempted by my pride and anger to hurt him back and keep it a secret. While I never contacted people I had previously been with,

I often felt justified in looking them up online to see where life had taken them.

Ashamed of my actions, I deleted my search history so my husband wouldn't find it. It started to become a habit, and I would look again, again, and again. When I would get caught, all I could argue was that it wasn't like I had cheated on him like he did on me—what a messed-up mentality! During this time, I began letting go of God and gripped tightly to my pride. I wanted pain for pain and insecurity for insecurity. I was silently plunging myself into a darkness of despair. Wouldn't it have been better to remain Christ-like instead of trying to take part in the destruction that was unfolding before us?

This terrible mistake is a clear example of how failing to draw closer to God results in clinging to earthly desires—pride, anger, lust, etc. On top of the affair, my marriage suffered greatly as a result of my sinful nature and lack of faith. It wasn't until repenting from choosing myself over Jesus, that I was set free from my bondage. Only then did it become possible to begin restoring and healing my marriage. I had to stop being lukewarm whenever I was tempted and plant myself in the Lord.

Reading Scripture reminds us of God's love and promises for us. Just as Jesus's life demonstrated how to stand steadfast in God's truth, we should also combat these battles by equipping ourselves with God's armor. When lies start creeping in and try to sink their teeth into your spirit, we must be prepared to discern and resist your adversary. We must align our thoughts with His word.

This Holy Spirit-led perspective is a special anointing that cannot be found anywhere else. That is why many new-age ideologies fight hard to get you to love yourself and put yourself first. Hence, many people in today's society cannot grasp the concept of forgiving someone for cheating, but we were not designed to make ourselves our own gods. We were and are created in God's image to glorify Him. And through our unfortunate and unforgettable circumstances, God works miracles by creating a bridge to connect those who have gained victory over infidelity in their marriage and those who are searching for a reference point to discover healing.

It is here, at the feet of Jesus, where He is glorified. When all feels lost, and nothing makes sense, Christ establishes His purpose through your experiences so that you can have victory and share that victory with others. Without the mind of Christ, forgiving is unattainable. Contrary to what the world says about an affair being a blessing in disguise: "You merely were shown you were investing your life and time into the wrong person." It is a blessing in disguise because the Lord has kept His word to protect you by exposing what has been done in the dark and bringing it into the light (Luke 12:2-3). Allowing this realization to resonate deeply within you instills clarity and peace of mind.

God has always been and always will be on the throne of grace. He loves and cares for you so much that He died on the cross for our sins. In that, we are called to love and forgive those around us—especially the ones who have violated our love, trust, and respect.

BEING IMMOVABLE

One specific trigger that kept me crippled for over a year was driving by where the affair occurred. This trigger was close to home, literally, which made driving in that vicinity a burden. For a while, before knowing the exact location, I became fixated on wanting to know where it happened. I was winded and filled with heartache every time I drove past it. Once I learned that information, my fixation shifted to anger.

Corey and I could be having an amazing day together when, all of a sudden, we're passing by the area on the highway, and I would sink into darkness. My eyes would drift toward the window, haunted by the past. Then, in a matter of seconds, the joy ride was over. My hand would pull away from Corey's as if it had a mind of its own.

While he questioned what he did wrong or what was the matter, all I could say was, "Nothing." How could I go from pure bliss to torment so quickly? I didn't know how to break loose from the constant cycle that was suffocating me. I became desperate, yearning for emotional stability in Jesus Christ.

I needed to become immovable.

The instability of my emotions caused both an internal and external conflict that I wanted no part of. So I did the only thing I had the energy to do—I drew close to God. Drawing close to Him equipped me with the spiritual dominion and strength to resist the Devil. Which, in return, helped me overcome debilitating thoughts through the power of forgiveness and praise.

> "But thanks be to God, who gives us the victory through our Lord Jesus Christ. Therefore, my beloved brethren, be steadfast, immovable, always abounding in the work of the Lord, knowing that your labor is not in vain in the Lord." (1 Cor. 15:57-58)

I was not spiritually grounded in how God desired me to be, nor in how I longed to be. It wasn't until I let go of wanting to be in control that He was able to reign in my heart. Thanks to Him for being an immovable God because He gave me direct access to gain emotional stability. Now, I no longer have to worry when the Devil tries to attack my mind. All I have to do is confidently speak Jesus's name over myself, and peace is with me.

PRAISING IN SUFFERING

Think back on what your life was like before knowing this new reality. Were you suspicious and praying for answers, or were you living your life normally and praying for protection? Maybe someone you confided in for spiritual direction was praying for you. Whatever the case, God has fulfilled the promise to protect you (Isa. 41:10) by bringing you the truth you deserve.

How exactly is finding this out a blessing?

Well, imagine you have lived a long and fulfilling life with your spouse, and he dies without ever telling you the truth. Or, maybe his last dying words are, "I cheated," to finally tell you the truth before he's gone forever. These examples are horrible ways to find out your marriage has suffered from adultery! It is better to be told or find out sooner so that you both can reconcile, should both parties be willing.

Here are six reasons why finding out can be a blessing:

1. If your husband openly admits his mistake, it is a genuine sign of remorse, which is healthy when it's followed through with change.
2. It reveals heart issues and pain points in your marriage that you both need improvement.
3. Committed couples who remain married will have better chances of communicating.
4. You will learn many lessons about forgiveness.
5. You both will reap the spiritual, emotional, and physical benefits of choosing to stay together.
6. Lastly, it can strengthen your faith and personal relationship with God.

While this list is not exhaustive, use these as a starting point for accepting that this unveiling could benefit your family. Be encouraged that something good can come from it. Remember, we serve a mighty God. A powerful revelation about His ability to make beauty out of the ugliest of situations is found in the book of Isaiah.

> "'To console those who mourn in Zion, to give them beauty for ashes, the oil of joy for mourning, the garment of praise for the spirit of heaviness; that they may be called trees of righteousness, the planting of the Lord that He may be glorified.' And they shall rebuild the old ruins, they shall raise up the former desolations, and they shall repair the ruined cities, the desolations of many generations." (Isa. 61:3-4)

The Lord wants to give you beauty in exchange for the dark days you are facing. Be confident that you can come before your

God, ask intentional questions, and pray intentional prayers. Should you find yourself needing direction on what to pray for and how to begin drawing closer to God, consider these things: Say a prayer of thanks to the Lord for your family, God's grace and mercy, peace of mind, salvation, and His faithfulness to you in delivering His promises.

Then pray over your family, your mind, and your spouse's mind. Rebuke the wiles of the Devil, pray over your home, speak in tongues while walking through your house and pray that God will close doors to all evilness at work against you. Ask the Lord to set your face like flint (Isa. 50:7) and instill strength within you and your husband to help you contend for your marriage. Renounce all evil thoughts and words, spoken and unspoken. Pray for dominion and that He will have a special covering over your home.

After this, begin taking actionable steps toward those prayers. You can do this by reading God's word every morning and throughout the day, listening and singing worship songs (because claiming victory over your life goes a long way), creating a prayers list, writing in a daily journal or save new revelations and ideas on a Google Doc file about what God has placed in your heart to encourage you, and intercede for others who are going through what you are.

It's no secret that finding out about an affair will bring anyone to an extremely desperate place. I find this to ring true, especially because an affair can feel like a marital loss one must mourn. No longer could we say that after marriage, we never slept with anyone again. The most special part of our intimacy was violated, and I felt robbed. Personally, having discovered this, I was overcome with a feeling of loss and grief. All I could think about was my husband had broken his vow to keep our marriage sacred, and we could never change that.

I was desperate for some kind of solace in the Lord's strength as I tried to move forward in our marriage. Thankfully, in the book of Habakkuk, we can find a great example of what it looks like when we choose to rely on God during times of desperation. In this chapter, we see Habakkuk crying out to God in frustration and confusion as to why He would let Israel suffer under the hand of the wicked (Hab. 1:2-4), and then we see the Lord respond to him with hope and prophecy. This promise ultimately brings Habakkuk a strength like no other—not even strength that he could find inside himself—because *only* the power of God can perfect us in our weaknesses (2 Cor. 12:9).

The word of God brings genuine comfort in the midst of our most challenging circumstances. Instead of resisting and fighting with God, Habakkuk demonstrated humble faith during his trials. His faith and surrender enabled him to find solace in Jesus. Attempting to find comfort in human wisdom and earthly things will only lead us away from our maker and down a path of destruction. By turning to Jesus, we discover the joy of knowing God is with us no matter where we are or what we're facing.

Suffering and adversity will continue to sift us as wheat until we are caught up in the sky, but until then, what do *you* do in testing times?

While choosing to remain steadfast can certainly be challenging, it is also unfulfilling to seek answers to our feelings or situations. This is why I believe Habbakuk steers us to the unchanging word of God as our reference point. During this time of uncertainty, we can make wise decisions by grounding ourselves in His truth by choosing to believe and pursuing His goodness—instead of giving way to temptations that comprise our values. Habakkuk's unwavering faith is a great testimony of God's sufficiency being enough for any person's life. Even though we lack favorable conditions, we can find joy in knowing and being saved by Him.

That is because the Lord alone is enough to sustain us when all else is crumbling around us. Our Savior provides strength when we are weak, joy in despair, sustains us through every trial, and brings healing to our brokenness (Ps. 147:3). The great thing about our God is we can triumph and bring glory to Him by casting our anxieties upon Him, trusting in His provision, as we navigate through life's heartaches.

Have you noticed that generations Z and Alpha are ironically hypersensitive people who struggle to understand and relate to

Jesus's sufferings? If you discuss suffering with individuals among these groups, you will likely be met with people who cannot grasp the concept of forgiveness, let alone count their suffering as joy.

Anyone who observes this will also find that hardships push many away from God rather than closer to Him. Yet, it is in these time-sensitive moments when we are tested that character is formed. That is why we should aim to resist giving way to cultural pressure that says we don't need to forgive and stay married. The forming of good character is crucial to all lives because it determines one's values, virtues, and emotional responses.

> "My brethren, count it all joy when you fall into various trials, knowing that the testing of your faith produces patience. But let patience have its perfect work, that you may be perfect and complete, lacking nothing." (Jas. 1:2-4)

An article I read said this, "Gifts and abilities may open doors, but character will determine what we do once those doors are open."[2] I believe this to be of significance because genuine Christian character is formed when you surrender to Christ's plan and purposes for your life. That is why we should strive to mirror what Peter says about counting it all joy when we fall into suffering because our praise and worship draw us closer to God.

Drawing closer to God means resisting the Devil. We need to be so locked in with the Lord that we are immovable in the principles of our faith when our adversary flings fiery darts to knock us down. In order to do so, we have to practice resisting the Devil, maintaining a heart of forgiveness, and embracing a spirit of praise.

I am forever grateful for my pastors and fellowship because of the special anointing they have. Remarkably, there was a recent sermon that edified my spirit regarding suffering and being immovable. It stressed that being immovable is to be spiritually

---

2. Milt Borah, "Character Is Important for Being a Christian," November 29, 2019.

grounded, especially in the face of opposition. When we know how to handle adversity, grief, and heartache after an affair, it shapes our character and equips us for the road ahead. Besides, what better place is there to be than in the arms of Jesus during times of suffering?

It is to our spiritual benefit to come to the Savior with faith-filled hearts because He knows all there is to know about the depths of them (Ps. 139:4). No matter the details of our circumstances, we can find total peace in drawing near to our maker by planting ourselves in His hands, which will organically produce fruit in our lives. Doing so will bring about good seeds that will disperse into your marriage. Plus, the decision to draw closer to God can bring forth growth to your marriage and lead you to recommit yourself to values you might have lost sight of along the way.

CHAPTER THREE

Recommitting to Values

What did you believe in before life became distorted? When drawing near to God, we are brought to a place where we must choose to recommit to our values—values we once held onto so tightly but have left behind along the way.

Before saying "I do," I made it clear to my husband that if we were to marry, divorce could not be an option; this was a joint agreement. We decided not to run away at the first sight of threat or danger. We made an informed decision based on each of our upbringings. (Easier said than done, I know.) We both came from broken homes that did not prioritize the nuclear family. Our absent fathers and parents' lack of commitment to each other negatively impacted how we carried ourselves in life. Hence, we have an intentional commitment to make a stand and choose to stay married, even during hard times.

This joint decision will forever change the trajectory of our lives, our children's lives, and their children's lives.

Many will argue this stance by pointing out, "No one should feel obligated to stay in a marriage after being cheated on just because they have kids together." And as much as those words might tickle your ear, that is one of the many lies the Devil wants you to believe (John 8:44). Keep in mind, he played a role in orchestrating this attack against your relationship and will go to any lengths to ensure total destruction.

CHRISTIAN VALUES IN CHANGING TIMES

When the Devil tries to manipulate you while you are in a vulnerable place, your next move must be made carefully. Therefore, I challenge you to go against the grain by consider doing the opposite of what the world says you shouldn't in this situation. Which is this: You *should* consider your children. You *should* consider your spouse. Most importantly, you *should* consider what God wants for you.

Yes, He wants you to be happy. Yes, you deserve to have peace. Yes, you deserve to be loved. But why is choosing to leave one of the most common solutions people turn to? Why do we live in a world full of self-pleasers? I dare suggest that, in most cases, divorce can be used as an easy way out. This is mainly true for people who think that running away from the violation will grant them total relief from the pain they feel of being married to the person who wronged them.

The issue with choosing to end a marriage immediately without attempting to reconcile is that it takes you further away from the opportunity for redemption. While it may seem like you are sparing yourself from pain by removing yourself from the equation, you would really only make it worse by robbing yourself of experiencing healing by confronting the matter head-on.

For the record, I don't mean it's easy to go through a divorce. I'm painfully aware of the courage and strength it takes anyone to end a marriage when it is necessary. What I am talking about is different. In that, divorce can be used as a self-pleasing mechanism to guard oneself against future trauma (minus the exceptions, of course). The truth is we like to cut corners in life, especially when the person we have made a life-long commitment to has burned us. So when we are robbed of the vow to keep the marriage bed undefiled and sacred, our fight-or-flight response prepares our body to take action. If not careful, anyone can make a decision during the heat of the moment that does not align with their values because circumstances can distort what we believe in.

Now, those who are dealing with repeat infidelity offenses, are married to someone who has willfully ended the marriage, or is in physical danger of being with their spouse are the exception and should seek out headship regarding separation. In these cases, divorce is not to be considered as self-pleasing or an easy way out but rather necessary due to circumstances that are beyond their control. Yes, Matthew 19:9 is the only time in Scripture where God provides couples a way out of marriage. However, what Jesus says is not designed to be a blanket statement.

In other words, we should not assume that divorce after adultery is one truth that applies to all people and their vast sets of circumstances. Though Scripture does show us that God hates adultery—and especially unrepentant adultery—it also shows us that He hates divorce.

> "For the Lord God of Israel says that He hates divorce, for it covers one's garment with violence." (Mal. 2:16)

Have you considered that God wants to help guide you in this journey? Are you praying enough to be able to discern and follow His direction for your life? Whether it's stay or go, I firmly believe that God's will for our lives is to *stay*. Of course, this looks like making a careful, thought-out, and prayerful decision considering all factors of *your* situation (Prov. 3:5-6, Prov. 19:21, Jer. 29:10-14). More often than not, choosing to stay married after infidelity benefits many long-term because the couple and their family can come out stronger from it.

It's like how diamonds are formed under intense pressure, becoming one of the strongest natural materials on Earth. Likewise, our marriages are being tested, and we can form stronger bonds with our spouses by choosing to stay married despite the many pressures we may face.

Choosing to recommit to your values will help your family in ways you might have never considered. Aside from the spiritual and emotional benefits it will bring you, it will also teach your children how to navigate and triumph through problematic seasons in life. It will teach them that, although things do not always go as planned and are not easy, through contending with the Lord and maintaining one's salvation, there is hope for what appears to be the most hopeless of circumstances. These virtuous qualities will be passed down through generations to come.

Although this stance is not the popular opinion you see on social media platforms, keep in mind that for decades, secularism has eroded the nuclear family that the Bible teaches. One statistic shows that "In 1970, nearly 70% of American adults ages 25 to 49 were living with a spouse and at least one [biological] child. As of 2021—the most recent year for which they have data—that's fallen to 37%."[3] Another is a classic work from the 90s that correlates a child's well-being to family disruption. The outcome of this study determines that divorce affects children worse than (parental) death, with nonmarital births taking the cake.

The high school dropout rate for children of divorced parents was 31%, and the teenage pregnancy rate was 33%.[4] This information not only demonstrates that the nuclear home was once a minority in the USA but that it negatively impacts kids. Divorce has become an epidemic over the last thirty years, and new research suggests that "Children of divorced parents may be more susceptible to mental health issues such as depression, anxiety, and a heightened risk of relationship difficulties in their adult lives."[5] All things considered, society's values are fading, and its effects are far-reaching, even influencing Christian culture.

Bear in mind that choosing to remain still in our marriage and contending for restoration brings glory to God. The benefits of this truth are that He liberates those who stand steadfast in His

---

3. Juliana Kaplan, "The American Nuclear Family Is Officially Over," September 16, 2023.

4. Sara McLanahan and Gary D. Sandefur, *Growing up with a Single Parent: What Hurts, What Helps*, 1996.

5. Shaheen & Gordon Attorneys at Law, "Understanding the Impact of Divorce on Children." January 31, 2024.

presence amid adversity (Ps. 37:12-13). Christ brings stability, and He is our anchor. We are never more like Christ than when we commit ourselves for life to an imperfect person. As we know, Jesus did this for humanity, and nothing is perfect about us.

As born-again Christians, we must have good expectations of our future. Hope in the middle of a time of crisis and tragedy is what creates stability in our souls. God is not a liar, and He wants to bring His promises to pass for you, even if you have lost hope in the midst of your trial. Trust Him to bring you and your spouse out of this place of torment and allow God to make something beautiful out of what has become defiled and feels so ugly.

BUILD YOUR HOUSE ON THE ROCK

My husband and I travel frequently for his job. Every time we traveled out of state in 2023, we would get caught in terrible weather. First, it was a snowstorm on the way to Upstate New York, then we drove through a hurricane warning on our way to Miami, Florida, and the list goes on. Naturally, I was terrified every time Corey got called out for work because we never knew what to expect from the weather conditions for our trip. Over time I noticed I grew more fearful because of each negative experience from before.

Whether it was rain, snow, fires, or hurricanes, our lives were at the mercy of God's creation. No matter how safe Corey drove, we had no control over the severe rainfall, slippery roads, and wind gusts. Although I trusted him to drive carefully, my faith was in Jesus to get us to our destination safely—He was, and is my firm foundation. We always pray for traveling grace before a long trip, but sometimes I find myself praying the entire drive if the weather takes a turn for the worst.

By God's grace, we arrived at our destinations safely every time, even despite unexpected car troubles that occurred. I strongly believe that praying to Jesus, listening to songs of worship, and tuning into sermons have contributed to the peace I found during those uncertain moments. Likewise, when the storm of unfaithfulness comes beating outside our home, we better do more than hope that we have the right foundation. We need to re-evaluate and ensure our faith is still built on the Rock; God's foundation.

Without it, what would happen to our homes? The parable of the two foundations gives us a clear understanding of the differences between a faulty and a firm foundation (Matt. 7:24-27). For those who build their house on the rock, their homes will stand strong and endure the storms. Opposed to those who build their house on the sand, their homes will surely fall to complete destruction.

Initially, when the storm began for us, I put faith in myself. I demonstrated this by needing to be in control. I fell victim to the chaos around me and became distracted by our marital problems. Did I mean for that to happen? No, but it did and it is actually scary to think of how easily that can happen to any of us without even knowing it.

Having a faulty foundation put my marriage more at risk of failure because it made me anxious, angry, bitter, insecure, etc., which all affected the way I treated Corey. My lack of faith in the Lord separated me from the Christian values I had once held onto so tightly. Since my feelings dictated my decisions, like a flag waves in the wind, it made establishing boundaries hard. Being fickle was something that needed to change right away if we were going to move forward in our relationship. That is because fickleness would get in the way of establishing boundaries that would honor God.

These are some connections between recommitting to values and the urgency of having the right foundation. Take caution of how the affair has affected your faith. Ask yourself: What am I putting my faith in during this season of life? Have I found peace in the midst of this fierce storm? If you find yourself breaking apart in the sand, God wants to help you and give you the strength needed to weather this storm victoriously.

ESTABLISHING BOUNDARIES

A part of recommitting to values involves setting necessary boundaries. Consider this: healthy boundaries start with strong values.

In other words, if you lose sight of your values, it is possible that you will struggle to set clear boundaries. Since my marriage was built on fornication, I later realized our values were weak. They were weak because we had failed to establish boundaries—what a big mistake that was.

Therefore, I now stress to others how crucial it is to set boundaries early in their relationships in the hope that it will help them avoid unwanted circumstances in marriage. Though we did things backward in our case, I am glad we instilled boundaries nonetheless; better late than never. As Christians, we should always be seeking God's wisdom after an affair. His direction will guide you in making choices that align with His will and plan for your lives. A faulty foundation hindered me from getting advice early on in our marriage from my headship or church family on what appropriate boundaries should have looked like in our situation.

My fickleness contributed to a lack of firmness. I set boundaries but never followed through with the consequences when lines were crossed. Since then, I've learned that my actions do not need to be dictated by fear and that letting my yes be yes and my no be no is a part of trusting and obeying God. If I had only adhered to the boundaries we set after the first texting incident, it could have spared our marriage unnecessary heartache months later because Corey would have been confronted with the weight of his consequences immediately.

Believing God wants to protect me through my obedience was something I could not grasp then but I understand now. Is that you? Needless to say, establishing boundaries is tough. It is so tough that we may rather avoid it than confront it. Here are some other ideas on boundaries you can begin implementing immediately, and encourage your husband to meet:

- Being direct about your needs and feelings respectfully, regardless of whether you feel angry or in spite, can go a long way in strengthening your communication and respect for one another.

RECOMMITTING TO VALUES

- Encourage him to capture his thought life (Rom. 12:2), halt communication with other women, and refrain from being alone with women who are not related to him.
- Emphasize wearing your wedding rings proudly at all times (blue-collar workers are an exception during work hours).
- Use clear language that does not attack your spouse or guilt trip them, while still targeting areas of previous weaknesses to hold them accountable in the future. (Be sure to set boundaries for yourself if you have fallen into temptation during this time, as well.)

Moreover, if your spouse used to hide his phone from you or has a password he didn't share with you, you can discuss the importance of being able to have full access to his phone and social media. At the same time, it is equally important to ensure we don't abuse that access and become tyrants. Communication with your spouse about how each of your choices contributed to the violation should humble and avert you from being controlling.

In our case, I struggled with looking up old lovers on social media. When I was reminded of my wrongdoings, I was confronted by the fact that I am an imperfect person too. Proving that I equally owed Corey the same respect to set clear boundaries on my behalf that would hold me accountable. For me, this looked like getting counsel from my headship so that Corey would be protected from potential repeat offenses on my part and so my relationship with God would remain guarded.

Sometimes, dealing with a husband's sexual sin confronts us with our own set of addictions that need to be rid of. In our case, I identified my addictions as such.

Setting boundaries should never be about responding out of vengeance, but about responding out of love. This is not the time to control your husband but to discuss with him that it is wrong to treat you the way he has been treating you. It is communicating that because of your love and respect for him and your self-respect, you cannot and will not allow them to continue hurting you in that way.

During the first year of battling these issues, I could set a boundary alright, but I wasn't doing it with the right heart. I learned that constantly checking his phone, keeping him on a short leash, and monitoring his location created an oppressive environment. There is a drastic difference between establishing boundaries and treating your husband like a child. Being a controlling wife is dangerous territory for many reasons, but primarily because your spouse may come to resent you for it.

After infidelity we often find comfort, or at least *think* we find comfort, in constantly checking our husband's phone. However, this can become an abuse of access, making us a controlling wife who strangles all possibilities of developing the trust needed to move forward. Remember, you are choosing to stay, so setting boundaries should be about proactive transparency and providing a level of structure for what will happen if these boundaries are violated again.

One boundary that is crucial to set and for your spouse to agree to is to end all forms of communication with the affair partner or partners. His ongoing cooperation and faithfulness will be proof that he is genuine in his decision to reconcile the marriage, which *should* encourage you to begin trusting him again.

I remember one day Corey got a call from his friend to help him with something, which wasn't a surprise since they were close friends and worked together. Most of the time the baby and I would tag along with him, but this time we stayed home and that bothered me. As he headed toward the door, I provoked an argument about whether to get him to take us with him or to stay. That was never a good idea, not even when my plan worked.

This is just one instance where my controlling behavior only made matters worse. This time Corey had enough. We went back and forth about how I felt like he wasn't spending enough time with us and how he felt like I was acting like his mother—always finding something wrong with what he was doing, which was true. Even though he was willing to respect the boundaries we placed, I was not satisfied with his efforts and went to extreme measures to ensure he wouldn't relapse.

This was not proactive transparency. This was me mistreating my husband for my benefit even though he was cooperating with the boundaries and being faithful. It was selfish, no matter how justified I felt. Corey already knew what was at stake, and it was exhausting trying to be in control and gather the shattered pieces of our marriage. After months of running through the same cycle, I finally stepped off the hamster wheel. It was then that I accepted trust played a critical role in the boundaries we were setting.

I had to allow him space to grow and demonstrate his seriousness in this new stage of our relationship. Otherwise, he would never feel comfortable expressing himself or sharing information with me, and that would have continued to hinder our marriage. That is why I let go of my lack of trust and bad attitude. I desperately wanted Corey to know that he could share his unfiltered thoughts with me and that I trusted him to make wise decisions, especially because his new behavior gave me no reason to distrust him.

Weeks into practicing this, I saw a difference in the atmosphere of our home. Months after practicing this I saw a difference in his willingness to communicate with me. Three years later, this decision still serves as a catalyst that has helped strengthen our love and respect for each other. The lesson learned? Trust and boundaries go hand in hand.

The boundaries you place will vary depending on your circumstances and church counsel's advice. Here are some additional healthy boundaries to consider that have worked for us: no lying and no poor treatment (which can and should go both ways), agreeing on consequences for crossing established boundaries, complete transparency (open access to each other's logins), avoiding secretive behaviors, and fostering trust through actions.

As long as you execute these with the right intentions and without dwelling excessively on the past, your spouse will have two choices: choose to do what is necessary to honor your boundaries or revert to pursuing unclean interests. In the event that it ends up being the latter, you should follow through with the course of action you have chosen to keep yourself safe. Hopefully, the re-evaluation you do will result in a change of heart for both of you. So, aim to stay true to your values and establish clear boundaries, which should provide the opportunity for intervention, change, and healing to begin.

WHISPERS OF DISCOURAGEMENT

Everything in this world will tell you nothing good can come out of your marriage anymore because "the marriage bed has been defiled" or that there is no hope for your spouse to change; "once a cheater always a cheater." Many in today's modern-day society will encourage you to leave while you can, but now is not the time to lose hope, act on emotion, or become isolated.

It is common for others to see a woman choosing to stay as a sign of weakness and dependency; whether that be economically, familial, or emotionally related. It can be misunderstood as a woman who is "accepting" or "allowing" their spouse to have an affair, but of course, there are limitations and there must be boundaries set within the marriage. Ultimately, staying and focusing on healing and restoration in your relationship can be a great sign of strength. Of course, all credit is due to God in that department, however, the truth is that a woman doesn't just bow down and "accept" this violation. Rather, she finds refuge and strength in her God to help her overcome this adversity—which is far from weakness.

In cases like these, there is no better time than now to resist the strategies from Hell. By recommitting ourselves and our values to the Lord, we can model the behavior of David, the Psalmist. He also encountered people who were involved in wicked behavior. It's notable that David advises God's people to respond with stillness, patience, and faith instead of responding poorly.

While David's instruction may seem impossible or out of reach, it is truly not as far as one may think. It's quite tangible because Christ has made these spiritual resources readily available to us. So that you can have victory when everything around you crumbles to the ground, essentially, you can gain victory by fighting your spouse's sin with delight.

Psalm 37 has great advice uniquely designed to help Christians navigate difficult seasons. This is where the idea of fighting sin with delight comes from (Ps. 37:4). Not only is this scripture comforting and reassuring, but it's a promise. The promise is that God can give you the desires of your heart if you choose to delight yourself in Him.

How can a person have faith when all hope seems lost? Spend more time with the Lord during morning prayer and anytime throughout the day when you sense your flesh is trying to rise within you: Study scripture, worship Him by listening to godly music as you go about your day (a song I played on repeat was Fear is a Liar by Zach Williams), reach out to like-minded believers from your congregation, or better yet step out of your comfort zone and arrange time to fellowship or talk with your headship. Having others pray for you, pray over you, fast with you, and pour out nourishing words into your life will edify you like nothing else will.

Don't believe the lie that you don't need to be involved with the church or surrounded by other believers. Your headship and the prayers and support of your church family are absolutely indispensable.

By putting faith into action, you demonstrate your trust in the Lord, and He will take up your yoke so you can make it (Job 13:15). Your salvation, your marriage, and your family will come out better for it. Every day, you should live with the expectation that there will be a blessing tomorrow. You can have the victory in this situation. Otherwise, when we lack expectation it brings isolation and isolation yields sin. Don't be discouraged; He is our reference point, refuge, and soul stabilizer.

It's also important to consider the change in values we expect from our unsaved spouses. How can an unsaved man or woman change when they don't share your spiritual convictions? Two words: morals and conviction. I strongly believe the Lord knew what He was doing when He instilled morals in all mankind. And while mankind has proven to grow cold and detached without salvation, wars, brutal murders, etc. That does not mean all hope is lost for those who are unsaved.

As humans, God has implanted in us the ability to understand the basic laws of morality and conviction. Essentially, the inner sense of rightness about our behavior and being made aware of one's sin resonates even with those who are lost. Jason K. Ritchie puts it like this, "Sometimes, unfortunately, a person needs to experience the consequences of lusting to address the issue."[6] Like any other individual our spouses have a heart, emotions, and more often than not, love their families. Similarly, spouses who make the mistake of committing adultery might also want to reconcile what they have caused damage to, in hopes of improving themselves so that their marriages work out and they keep their families together.

HOPE IN CHOOSING TO STAY

My point is, at the end of the day, we are all sinners, and the only thing separating a Christian from a non-Christian is the blood of Jesus Christ. While I am a firm believer that being a good person doesn't get anyone into Heaven, I also believe that morals and conviction can help deter unsaved individuals from committing repeated offenses, especially when their families and marriages are hanging in the balance. In reality, change comes because we care and are willing to do whatever we can to be different; that is a change of heart (1 John 3:18).

As you choose to walk in this truth, you will reap the benefits of His promises—and He always delivers. We can find hope in Jesus for healing and discovery of a marriage that is even more satisfying than the one we experienced before. The Bible gives us hope for our unsaved spouses in various Scriptures; these particular two are my favorite:

---

6. Jason K. Ritchie, *Oh God Why Can't I Stop: How God's Response to Failure Conquers Shame and Paves Your Way to Victory*, 2022.

RECOMMITTING TO VALUES

> "For the unbelieving husband is sanctified by the wife, and the unbelieving wife is sanctified by the husband: else were your children unclean; but now are they holy. But if the unbelieving depart, let them depart. A brother or a sister is not under bondage in such cases: but God hath called us to peace." (1 Cor. 7:14)

> "Wives, likewise, be submissive to your own husbands, that even if some do not obey the word, they, without a word, may be won by the conduct of their wives." (1 Pet. 3:1)

The hope in recommitting ourselves to our values (God's will) is that He will save our spouses one day. Likewise, recommitting to our values includes praying for our signficant other daily and praying for our enemies (Phil. 4:6-7). Oh, what a joyful thought that our meekness, obedience, and prayers have the dominion to win their souls for Jesus. However, when choosing commitment, it is pivotal to recognize the resistance that comes to work against you to discourage you from making choices that please God and honor your Christian values.

The Devil is always waiting for an opportunity to bring division and create an oppressive environment. That is why it's made so easily accessible in today's world to just walk away. But when Christ begins softening your heart to forgive your spouse, when you let go, you finally experience that pure liberation your broken heart has longed for. This is why the Devil works so hard at keeping you lost in painful memories; so he can rob you of healing and joy! Beat him at his own game by taking dominion over your circumstances so you are prepared to resist him and the lies ahead.

CHAPTER FOUR

Rejecting the Devil's Lies

You are not enough and the Devil won't let you forget it. Maybe you have even gone to extreme measures to be someone you are not in an attempt to satisfy, what you believe are your husband's desires. After recently reading Allie B. Stuckey's book, *You Are Not Enough (And That's Okay): Escaping the Toxic Culture of Self-Love*, I have come to understand, more deeply, the fallacy of self-love and all its strategies—one of the Devil's most popular lies.

Specifically, the notion that we *are* enough is flawed because we will never find true satisfaction within ourselves. We see this especially when an affair takes place and all we can think about is how inadequate we are during this challenging season. The concept of self-love leads people to believe that our earthly desires can be fulfilled without a Savior. Though many people around you may have good intentions when they tell you that you need to put yourself and your needs first, it's crucial to recognize the difference between self-worth and self-love.

LIE #1: SELF-LOVE WILL PROTECT YOU FROM YOUR MARRIAGE

That said, practicing self-love, especially after your marriage is hit with adultery, can be extremely precarious. We must acknowledge a fine line between self-worth and self-love. The Bible tells us that self-worth is given to us by God and that He provides us with strength and all that we need to live a godly life or how to navigate trials when we need direction—it helps us know who we are in Christ (Ps. 139:13-14). On the contrary, God warns us about becoming lovers of ourselves in the last days, "But understand this, that in the last days there will come times of difficulty. For people will be lovers of self, lovers of money, proud, arrogant, abusive, disobedient to their parents, ungrateful, unholy" (2 Tim. 3:1-2).

While the Bible does encourage us to love our soul enough to contend for goodness and truth, it also calls us to beware of the spirit of self-love in today's modern world. With appropriate boundaries and godly confidence, we can be mindful of our well-being and avoid putting ourselves in unhealthy situations.

When our hearts are healing after an affair, the Devil will tempt us to make a decision that mirrors a secular discourse of self-affirmation by putting yourself first, which is supposed to protect you from future suffering. The "love yourself" mentality is merely a shorthand for assuaging a troubled conscience. In this case, the expression can be used as a way of denying the hurt inflicted on us by avoiding reconciling with our husbands. If that's what's happening, we should acknowledge the reality of our circumstances: our mistakes and our spouse's mistakes, our sin and our spouse's sin, our regrets and our spouse's regrets, and each of our hurts. Taking time to analyze these things carefully is not self-betrayal—it's a chance to try again and make changes.

The last thing we should be doing is allowing this self-love notion to rob us of a second chance at making amends with our significant other or depending on ourselves to be good enough for them. Neither of the two work and will only cause destruction. Looking back now, I can recall where I left the door cracked for the

Devil to continue to invade my home and inflict torment on me by bringing in insecurity for not being the other woman, looking like the other woman, etc. Back then, the idea of not being enough felt like such a bad thing, but it isn't. I had to combat the Devil's manipulation by rediscovering a truth I already understood: that it is okay not to be enough—because God is enough!

This realization brings perfect peace, which is why the Devil works tirelessly to get us to believe otherwise. Since our confidence comes from the Lord, we can certainly find it in Him during our trials.

> "For if our heart condemns us, God is greater than our heart, and knows all things. Beloved, if our heart does not condemn us, we have confidence toward God." (1 John 3:20-21)

We can find confidence in Christ instead of in ourselves. He is our identity, and His power shines through our weaknesses, so we don't have to be overcome by shame and embarrassment of our flaws, struggles, and imperfections. So when the Devil insists on telling you that you are not enough, remember the truth: you are not enough, but God is, and through Him, we can find confidence like no other.

Instead of leaning on ourselves to find our identity and worth, which always leads to turmoil, we should be leaning on Christ and finding fulfillment in how He views us. Romans 5:8 says, "But God demonstrates his own love for us in this: While we were still sinners, Christ died for us." We are blessed and highly favored that Jesus loves us, not because we are attractive or try so hard to make ourselves good enough for Him, but simply because He loves us.

Oh, what a refute to the notion of self-love and a liberating thought for you and me. Again, there is a fine line between self-love and having confidence that only Christ can instill through providing you with identity. As women living in this day and age, it is easy to allow negative attitudes to rule over the Holy Spirit because society has told us that women with a submissive, quiet, and lowliness spirit mean they're doormats, especially when a wife chooses to stay married after infidelity, which is far from the truth.

The meanings of permissiveness and submission have been misconstrued so much that people associate the two together. However, being permissive drastically differs from submitting to a husband. For instance, being permissive involves being quiet and codependent while letting the husband rule out dominance. While submission requires honor and respect; it is willingly coming under the authority of another.

These truths go against the grain of modern feminist ideologies and are different from God's biblical elevation of women. "The problem with feminism itself is that it sets up a *false idea* of what it means to defend the dignity of women," Isa Ryan put in her article.[7] This narrative of oppression, especially in situations like this, shows a lack of faith in God's ability to reconcile a broken marriage. While I understand the idea of staying married after an affair is another fine line regarding oppression, when remorse is met with change, there can be real hope for the submissive wife and her broken marriage.

What we see in the world today are feminist and new-age ideologies that stir resistance and ungodliness. They tell you that it is better to leave your marriage because there's no change in sight; your husband is no longer worthy of being "a keeper" because of the affair. But friends, if we were only long-suffering and patient for God's still small voice to guide us, He would bring us to the other side.

Worldly wisdom leaves out God's goodness and faithfulness. It ignores His mighty ability and places a burden on ourselves. May we never forget that sometimes, to get over a storm, you have to go through it. We should not focus on the pain that comes from our current decisions—to stay or go—but rather think about the impact our decisions will have on our futures and those around us.

---

7. Isa Ryan, *The failing logic of feminism and the "red pill,"* October 4, 2023.

UNSOLICITED REMINDERS

Aside from my weaknesses, the Devil also loves reminding me of my husband's failures from the first year of our marriage. There were many times I caught my spouse texting other women and extended forgiveness. He often said he would stop talking to them but failed to. Finally, after months of patience and quietness from God, he did. My husband changed his mind after he repented and confessed to committing adultery; it was as if a switch had turned on and remained on even after he drifted away from God and the church. Since then, the Lord has worked a miracle in our marriage by touching my husband's heart and showing us how to love each other in a way we never saw our parents do. I am grateful Corey has demonstrated a tangible change in our relationship and has positively expressed new behaviors and attitudes toward marital commitments since then.

Today, my husband is learning how to love me fiercely, only *after* experiencing my forgiveness for adultery. He does this by communicating temptations with me and talking about the steps he takes to combat unwanted thoughts or emotions. For instance, when a woman who is dressed immodestly walks in his direction, Corey chooses to look away (Matt. 5:29). Or if a woman tries to make a pass at him, he rejects their efforts, informs them he is married and makes it a priority to let me know what occurred right away.

He has also exemplified this by sticking to his values since we began the recovery process. Before I had removed myself from using Snapchat, he had not reciprocated—as I would later find out why. However, two years later, he removed himself from entertaining Snapchat and other applications. Putting up this wall benefited our marriage, as seen in the book of Nehemiah. Although walls are typically referred to as barriers that we need to break down, like those that block you from your spouse, I'm referring to the kind that guard your heart and marriage so that the outside world cannot stain it nor separate it.

Realizing where his weaknesses were and placing boundaries to protect himself from falling were small yet gigantic changes that confirmed his commitment to healing our marriage.

Despite the Devil's efforts to remind me of my husband's mistakes and imperfections, I had to come to an understanding that my spouse has his sin struggles just as I have mine. This constant reminder of my husband's mistakes caused me to often struggle with insecurity, torment, and the fear of being cheated on again. I had to constantly remind myself of the decision I was making (to stay) so that I could begin rejecting Satan's lies, trusting in God instead of holding my decision to stay over my husband's head.

I had to reject the fiery darts from Hell that were setting my heart ablaze: Every time I would randomly think unsettling thoughts of insecurity, fear, anger, and depression. I had to resist the Devil no matter how sad, lonely, and upset I felt because the Devil is a liar who wants us to believe our spouses are incapable of commitment after adultery!

A lot of the time, our feelings get in the way of making transformative progress. There is no doubt marinating in my feelings would have led me to surround myself with people who could have negatively influenced me by giving way to my emotions. For example, I'm sure you have seen or heard of wives who speak down to their husbands, speak negatively about their situation, or go out and party to "blow steam." I purposely avoided these things because I understood that to rebuild our marriage I needed to reject temptations and the Devil's lies. Though finding comfort in the wrong places and the wrong people appears enticing, there is nothing outside of the will of God that will bring us lasting peace of mind.

Simply put, no matter your husband's mistakes, you have to choose forgiveness daily and confidently rebuke the Devil when he tries to trip you up; while the appropriate boundaries are in play of course. Don't you know you have full authority in Christ to rebuke Satan? You should be exercising this dominion as often as necessary without fear of reproach (Isa. 51:7) because Satan is a stumbling block that needs to be removed from your way. There's no doubt *if* you will get attacked; it's a matter of *when*. So, when the next attack sneaks up on you, it's important to remember that you are equipped to resist his tactics.

LIE #2: HE'S STILL LYING

No matter how much time has passed after the affair, the Devil will attempt to trick you into believing your spouse is dishonest since he's done it before. The fear of being unable to make your husband tell the truth, or not having control over everything, only creates doubt about his integrity and whether or not he is still keeping secrets. After discovering videos in a secret folder during our first year of marriage, I felt extremely confident that one recording included my husband and her.

For two years, the Devil was relentless in getting me to believe a lie. In my mind, it only made sense that it was him—and man, did that Devil know where to strike a cord since we were both recovering from pornography addiction. However, it turned out that it was that woman with another man sharing her private images and videos with my husband. In a world where OnlyFans infects social media, pornography is made highly accessible to others, and my marriage was battling a similar disease of this sin firsthand.

I would be naive not to factor in the external elements that bombarded my marriage, which is why I am sharing this private incident with you. We should all face the fact that sexual immorality and pornography addiction are widespread in our societies, and can trickle into even the best of marriages at any stage of life. Unfortunately, our 21st-century ideologies and vices are strongly associated with these common practices that proved detrimental in my marriage; and many other marriages. So it would be wise to reflect on what external elements have influenced your spouse's decisions.

The images I saw were daunting and stained my perception of him for a long time. I constantly felt like my spouse was still keeping secrets from me after he had come clean about the affair. I constantly felt the need to dig for more. I went through his phone and his emails. Through his truck and clothes. Through phone records and location. The idea of him being dishonest robbed peace from me and made it harder for me to let go of the past. Due to these doubts, I refused to believe him when he told me countless times that it was not him in the video and that she sold footage of herself being intimate with men online.

In light of the history, I lost all trust in him and refused to accept his word—it meant very little to me then. The damage that was caused led me to grow increasingly fearful and doubtful of his honesty, creating a disconnect in our relationship and intimacy. Every so often, months would pass and I was still being triggered to question the validity of his word. The Devil manipulated me into believing his clever lie about that video because he knew that my husband's sin and my lack of trust were the perfect brew for division.

However, once he proved to stop watching pornography, talking to other women, and violent outbursts, Corey demonstrated self-discipline by controlling his emotions and remaining accountable for his private thoughts and inner struggles. As his faithful attributes grew consistent, I had to trust Jesus was sitting on the throne above it all. My duty as a Christian wife was to not grow weary in taking control over my spouse or marriage to embrace healing and to move beyond fear and doubt. I had to intentionally decide, and keep deciding, that I wasn't going to let the Devil have control over my mind and scare me into becoming a nagging and contentious wife—I had to give total control to God and His healing process.

The truth is that no matter how much time passes, the Devil will always try to sneak through an open door at any given time. We can find a balance by striving to be vigilant and casting our worries on the Lord. This is why praying every morning is paramount in resisting temptations of fear, doubt, resentment, and all other unholy things. In 2 Timothy 1:7, Paul reminds followers of Christ that He did not design us to be fearful. Instead, He has given us access to His power, love, and a sound mind.

These components are necessary to overcome the Devil, our adversary. If fear resonates within our hearts, we have to act quickly by walking in the truth of God's promises. We must boldly call on the Holy Spirit to be outpoured on us, choose to love our spouses daily, and accept the peace Christ has made available to us so we can have healthy minds.

Like Jesus used Scripture to fight off Satan's temptation, we too can have victory over the evil in ourselves and around us. As extreme as it may sound, small dilemmas like fear, doubt, and resentment are all tools of wickedness that prevent, even believers, from entering the Kingdom of God. Since God did not create us to live in such a way, living differently in any way is deemed as unrighteous in His eyes—no unholy thing can enter into Heaven. So why should we allow modern-day feminist ideologies and self-love culture to become idols at the expense of separating ourselves from God? Wouldn't you rather trust God instead of feeding a spirit of fear that fills your mind with lies? The Bible clearly says not to be lukewarm, or else we will be spewed out of His mouth; being a Christian means coming to the feet of Jesus daily, allowing Him to bring correction to our hearts of such sins, and having faith even in the darkest of circumstances.

LIE #3: SPIRIT OF REJECTION

Additionally, another major stumbling block the Devil will use to prevent you from forgiving is implanting the seed of rejection. Rejection was a perfect strategy to use against me in this crisis of my life because I had a history of rejection with my father and other relationships growing up. For years, I carried this spirit on me and coddled oppression like it was an inner child.

Then when I found Corey talking to women online and about his physical relationship with the other woman, I couldn't help but feel the spirit of rejection creep up on me again. The Devil is infamous for this; trying to get us sucked into oppressive cycles. And I can't lie, he almost hooked me another time too.

I felt like no one loved me—not even the one person who had vowed himself to me till death. Rejection victimized me into believing I was worthless and unwanted. I know this is something all of us have dealt with before, so let us consider the burden this spirit brings and how damaging it is to carry.

Embracing rejection and self-pity is like lugging heavy, dirty bags of sin around as if they are fashion accessories. We do it because we are comforted by ruminating over problems, craving sympathy from others, or feeling angry at the cards we've been dealt. If not careful, these issues will corrupt our lives, and rejection will begin to affect our spiritual outlook on life if it hasn't already. It wasn't until I accepted this problem as a demonic spirit, humbled myself before God's rebuke, and allowed Him to deal with my heart that I was able to reach my God-given capacity in everything I did, which was otherwise limited when I adapted to this spirit.

The spirit of rejection needs to be uprooted from our lives. It gives birth to destructive thoughts and emotions. Face it, whether we mean to or not, we often look at our lives through the lens of the past. But this will only lead to an inability to maintain healthy relationships with people and God. Not getting closure will make you an angry person. However, you can find freedom from this spirit once you understand that the past is not an excuse; it's an explanation that tells us where we need healing.

In Hosea 9:16, we are shown that a withered root can't produce good fruit. Quite literally, our innate need for love and acceptance is so strong that our actions amplify the rejection we've experienced. Thus, we need to address the spirit of rejection birthed from the affair and uproot it.

In Romans 8:38-39, Paul tells us that man's rejection is made so small in light of the truth that, through God's word, we have His eternal love and unconditional acceptance. This truth alone should be enough reason to forgive. However, if you still find yourself marinating in a pool of rejection, please consider this a gentle reminder that deadly emotions and their manifestations come at a lofty price.

LIE #4: WE CAN GIVE UP WHEN NO CHANGE IS IN SIGHT

It seems easy to give up when all we see is the sin birthed from an unclean heart, no hope seems to exist, and we're too weak to go on. But, we don't have to curl up in a ball and cut our losses over this trial, and we certainly don't have to be swayed by other people's opinions on how it would be better for us (the victim) to protect ourselves from any more hurt by leaving. Why should we be conformed to hopelessness when we are children of a high King?

The Devil has used a similar tactic before on Jesus at the Last Supper, leading up to His crucifixion. He used Peter as an instrument in order to rebuke Jesus from dying on the Cross for our sins (Matt. 16:21-23). Peter gave off the impression that the Lord was taking matters to the extreme by stating, "Far be it from You, Lord; this shall not happen to You!" and Jesus's response to Peter's rebuke was calling him Satan. Jesus had to discern, identify, and call out the offense of the Devil, even though he was using Jesus's disciple against Him. As the scripture continues, Jesus begins consulting His disciples by instructing them to deny themselves, take up their cross, and follow Him (Matt. 16:24).

Now, I am not suggesting that you call anyone the Devil for recommending divorce in this situation with your spouse, considering they have your best interest in mind. Although, I encourage you not to be afraid of being reproached by our adversary. What I mean by that is the Devil wants us to feel like forgiving our husbands for adultery is extreme, especially when all we see is ugly. But in certain circumstances, when a husband *shows* they are willing to work to save the marriage, throwing in the towel might not be the best solution for that couple.

A reproach from the Devil through people, our disappointment, and fears are only a few of the many things that can influence us into making decisions that we might later regret. Yes, the bed defiled is one of the most hurtful things someone could endure in marriage, but let us not forget that the Lord understands our pain. He, too, was betrayed and identifies with our struggles—this is what makes Him qualified to guide us and redeem our relationships. Our spouses are human beings, just like us, who are tempted to sin and sometimes disappoint us with their actions. Thankfully, we serve a God who will never disappoint us and who wants to heal our marriages and reconcile us to our spouses.

We can discard the notion that giving up when no change is in sight is acceptable by clinging to this truth, "He will keep you strong to the end, so that you will be blameless on the day of our Lord Jesus Christ" (1 Cor. 1:8). The good news is, when we are weak and feel insufficient, His strength is enough for us.

Once I let go of fear, I realized that my life and our future together were full of incredible love and possibilities. All I had to do was choose to stay and trust the plan God had planned for us ahead. Because of that, I started nourishing some critical things I had neglected at the start of our marriage when I failed to honor, respect, and uplift my husband. Of course, losing the purity of your marriage is still very scary—and I'm not mentioning *all* that's required to overcome this mindset shift—but too often, we look to our husbands as our source of identity and security.

However, doing that will only destabilize us if or when our husbands are gone (and odds are you aren't going to be stuck in this state of your marriage forever; at least, you shouldn't be). For me, going through this heartbreak has fundamentally changed the way I look at marriage. There are many other things in the garden of my life that demand more water and sunlight. As long as I look at my marriage from a birds-eye view instead of focusing on this painful mistake, God will see me through it, and I will be okay—and so can you.

Our hope in Jesus is that our faith should give us the courage to stand fast against hard times and the strength to defend the truth of the gospel, should our circumstances permit an opportunity for reconciliation. Hopefully, as we pursue sound judgment, others around us who have been hurt as we have will take notice, find hope in these truths, and persevere for change.

LIE #5: WE CANNOT FORGIVE THEM

When Satan tries to make you fall, he will always try to use you as your enemy in attempting to get you to believe that we cannot forgive them for what they've done. This is noticeably one of the biggest lies the Devil tries to use to bring division between us and our spouses, as well as between us and God. He wants us to believe that what they have done to us is unforgivable and beyond repair. Our adversary lurks around our homes, projecting a giant shadow of despair on the walls, leaving no room for forgiveness in sight when, in reality, he is so small compared to the God we serve. Forgiveness is attainable no matter how doomful the lies he tells us sound.

When all this occurred, I was backsliding for a season, then began faithfully attending church and serving Jesus again. Throughout that time, I heard many different things from different types of people. Not only had I heard that a man who cheats doesn't deserve forgiveness, but I had witnessed marriages that underwent adultery, chose to remain married, and lacked forgiveness. So, I climbed on a third boat that differed from the first two.

This third boat decided to stay married and believed forgiveness was right but encountered waves of difficulty pursuing *continual* forgiveness. This boat was special because it didn't know how to navigate continual forgiveness in a storm like this. Emotions of anger and confusion ruled over what I knew was God's will for my life, but I felt like I had zero control as holiness and joy faded away into the dark abyss of my marriage.

I longed to be a godly woman, but the bitterness I was growing toward my husband blocked me from healing and growth. I would go weeks lying to myself, acting like I was better than my husband since I wasn't the one who cheated, yet my heart was filled with the sin of hate inside. The Devil worked hard at getting me to believe that Corey was the one who needed forgiveness and not me. He handicapped me by making me think I was still a godly woman even though fear and unforgiveness were rotting my bones. He continuously brought back the memory of the initial hurt after discovering the affair so I could feel justified in my ungodly thoughts, attitudes, and behaviors toward my husband, but that should not have been so.

We forgive because we have been forgiven (Eph. 4:32). There should be no excuses. Though we are to be wise and careful when creating and maintaining healthy boundaries, we must forgive because Jesus forgave us. How can we say that we cannot forgive when God sent His only Son, Jesus Christ, to come to earth knowing He was called to live a sinless life and would have to die for the sins of all of humanity? If He came to earth in the flesh and forgave us for betraying and crucifying Him, how are we not capable of forgiveness toward those who betray us?

Forgiveness doesn't mean that those who have hurt us are getting away with betrayal. It means to let go of resentment and any claim to be compensated for the hurt or loss we have suffered.[8] Suppose you are struggling to forgive your husband and the woman who has done wrong to you. In that case, you may have allowed the Devil access into your heart (Matt. 5:44). One of the best ways to combat this stronghold is to fast and earnestly pray against these demonic attacks and potential heart issues (Matt. 17:21).

Now, you might wonder where you can find the strength to commit to forgiveness like that because you tried it, and it didn't last long. Allow me to say that you are right on track. However, let us not forget that we cannot forgive on our strength alone; we will *always* need Jesus. In the Bible, He shows us that a healthy boundary love looks like a sacrificial and selfless love that shows itself in action.

Although this list of five deceptions includes some of the Devil's main hitters, it is not exhaustive. The Devil will use any strategy to impart a spirit of division in our marriages, especially during the aftermath of infidelity. The good news is that there is hope in Jesus to win this battle. We can identify our reactions as holy or unholy by remaining prayerful and asking the Lord for discernment. Since we are imperfect people, the answer will almost

---

8. Los Angeles Christian Counseling, "Learning How to Forgive: 8 Steps to True Forgiveness," September 13, 2023.

always be unholy when dealing with bitterness, unbelief, self-pity, and self-love. Thankfully, Jesus is enough for us, through us, giving us the discernment and dominion to come against these demonic attacks.

CHAPTER FIVE

Forgiving Daily

What does one do when they don't want to forgive? Or perhaps what should someone do when they have forgiven their spouse while working tirelessly to resist the Devil, yet unwanted memories keep triggering unhealthy emotions? You check your attitudes and re-analyze your heart's condition by remaining accountable for forgiving your husband daily. If you want real transformation and to be liberated by God's power, then you must subject yourself to becoming more Christ-like. Not just once or now and then, but by forgiving every time the Devil targets you with attacks. Although we have already discussed forgiving the unforgivable, what about forgiving what we can't forget?

Remember what Jesus said to His disciples in Matthew 16:24. Similarly, forgiving your husband anytime you are challenged to revert to bitterness is an act that must be practiced daily. That means picking up your cross daily (1 Thess. 5:17); full surrenderance involves continual forgiveness, not half-hearted commitment. From the time you wake up and go to bed, you have to keep deciding to become more Christ-like. His powerful example of a sinless life demonstrates the importance of the need to forgive anytime someone hurts us or when thoughts try to hurt us. Jesus didn't hold the concept of forgiveness loosely—He grasped it tightly. He was intentional in action, and every word was up to the point of dying on that cross so that we could be forgiven of our sins. How much more does the Lord want us to do the same for our neighbors and spouses who afflicted us?

A 2023 study entitled Forgive, Let Go, and Stay Well shows that chronic diseases are rising with unforgiveness.[9] That is because there are undeniably indirect effects of unforgiveness and health. It says, "According to previous research, there is a correlation between forgiveness and a decrease in ruminative thoughts. Thus, forgiveness may reduce repetitive thoughts and enhance reflection, leading to better health. The purpose of this research was to test how positive forgiveness and reduced unforgiveness relate to health."

Additionally, it stresses Enright's definition of forgiveness as "A willingness to abandon one's right to resentment, negative judgment, and indifferent behavior toward one who unjustly injured us, while fostering the undeserved qualities of compassion, generosity and even love toward him or her."[10] I find this second definition interesting because it acknowledges that forgiveness coincides with fostering underserved qualities toward the person who did wrong to you. Forgiveness is more than saying you forgive; it requires us to be kind to one another and tenderhearted as Christ did for us (Eph. 4:31-31).

Forgiving your husband daily, in this way, will liberate you by breaking the chains of bondage in your marriage. Even more significantly, God will work in your husband's backslidden heart by using you as an example of His ultimate grace and mercy. There is no better advice than that of the Lord Himself. Deny yourself of all unholiness and pick up your cross.

This was a game-changer for me. As hard as it was to let go and give God the keys to my heart, I've reaped the benefits of remaining married since I decided to forgive my husband daily. It

---

9. Justyna Mróz and Kinga Kaleta, "Forgive, Let Go, and Stay Well! The Relationship between Forgiveness and Physical and Mental Health in Women and Men: The Mediating Role of Self-Consciousness." June 26, 2023.

10. Enright, In RD, and J. North. "Exploring forgiveness (pp. 46-62)." 1992.

is a decision I will never regret because it has redeemed me, and every day, I am grateful to reap and witness the blessing of my selfless decision because the love I have for my husband instills a deep sense of security within our child.

BEAUTIFUL MEMORIES

Ever since Aria was one year old, we have seen how she'd been comforted by us both remaining together and by each other's side. She shows us this by holding both of our hands—and not just any hand-holding. The kind that makes your heart flutter because you are reminded that all the sacrifices have been worth it. During these random moments when we sit beside her, she looks up at us with her big, chocolatey round eyes and gently taps and places her left hand, palm up, on her dad's arm. He then responds by grasping her hand, which signals her to extend her right hand to me and repeat those gestures in that same order until I, too, fulfill her nonverbal requests—to make her feel loved and secure. Her healthy expectations of having both her father and mother hold her hands and the gleaming smile that radiated on her face afterward put the cherry on top for us.

Other times, she would bring both of our faces together so we could plant a kiss on each side of her cheeks and then guide us with her tiny hands by uniting us above her head to kiss each other. As she tilted her head back to watch us follow through with planting a peck on each other's lips, she would begin to hysterically giggle while we made our way back to squishing her cheeks with kisses again until we got tired of the pain in our stomachs from all the laughter.

In many ways, our daughter worked as a glue between us in those two first years of marriage. Getting pregnant played a major role in making our decision to get married. Neither of us wanted her to grow up in a home without a father—we wanted so much more for her than we had experienced in our own lives. As the months passed and my belly grew, Corey would caress her and plant kisses over me (even though she would kick back to get him off of her). In those early moments between us, she innately grew attached to him.

When she was born after my emergency c-section, Corey met with her and the doctors at another hospital as they worked around the clock to help save our daughter's life. Our almost losing her was the first traumatic experience my husband and me had ever shared. He would sing Angel Baby by Rosie and The Originals to her while she slept all day due to the sedation. It was the same song he sang to her while she was in my womb. The lyrics, "Please never leave me blue and alone, if you ever go I know you'll come back home," brought comfort to us that she would make a full recovery and come home to us. (I always thought it was ironic how the song's meaning changed after discovering the affair; later, I began associating those lyrics with Corey.)

When she survived, sticking together meant ten times more than it had done nine months prior. We are forever grateful for the miracle God performed. Choosing to stay married and forgiving daily was something I knew I had to do, despite how hard it was. Our daughter was a survivor, and there was no way that either of us could just throw in the towel. I wanted us to fight like she fought to stay with us, and we did.

I would need to remind myself of this battle we overcame and the kind of father Corey was to our child. I would reanalyze how and why our childhoods and poor spiritual decisions led us to where we were then. Although these were not excuses for his behavior, they certainly were our realities. Choosing to forgive him daily was a decision I was making not only for myself but also for my daughter and our family as a whole.

The decision to stay married is priceless, and these actionable steps, taken from the living, breathing word of God itself, will guide you on your journey to redemption. He will lift you from the miry pit of destruction and restore a firm foundation within your life and marriage through forgiveness (Ps. 40:2). Remember, forgiveness isn't an act that just happens once, but continually.

WHEN BITTERNESS RESURFACES

I'm guilty of heating up on a forgiveness streak and then suddenly allowing myself to backpedal into a boiling pot of emotional sabotage. And then there I am, moving further and further away from victory and undoing all of the progress God had just carried me through. Truthfully, I am not sure why I would fall into self-destruction mode at random times. I can presume it might be due to the things I was exposing myself to then, like movies that I would watch that involved affairs or listening to songs that would talk down on men for cheating—Bust Your Windows by Jazmine Sullivan.

Small decisions like these have a major impact on our everyday walk with God. How can we walk in the Spirit while filling our hearts with such things? When I allowed myself to be entertained by meaningless and damaging entertainment, they would re-open doors that I kept praying for God to shut. It was counterproductive, really. Nonetheless, when I would find myself in this place, the Lord always brought me back to the scripture, "For what I am doing, I do not understand. For what I will to do, that I do not practice; but what I hate, that I do" (Rom. 7:15).

In light of that truth, I find it important to remain raw and honest with ourselves at all times. In Romans 7, we can find that even the mature believer struggles with sin; in our case, bitterness will constantly try to creep in. The Christian struggle is real! There is no need to be ashamed of the imperfections we face. Although we have been freed from sin's power, we still live under its strong influence. While we have good intentions to do the right thing (forgive and move on), we find ourselves doing the wrong thing (returning to unforgiveness) instead, without fully understanding why.

When we fail to trust God's plan and act on our fleeting emotions, we replant seeds of sin in our hearts. We must be careful that one day's worth of bottled-up emotions won't become next week's catastrophic disaster. Beware of bottling up unwanted emotions! Give your burdens to Christ the second you feel yourself falling short of His glory because, thankfully, we can find total freedom in His grace:

> "Looking carefully lest anyone fall short of the grace of God; lest any root of bitterness springing up cause trouble, and by this many become defiled." (Heb. 12:15)

HARMFUL EMOTIONS INFLICT PHYSICAL ILLNESSES

If we work against God there is no room for healing; and if we're too busy reverting to old sinful habits, our heart issues will manifest themselves into physical illnesses. In books like *Deadly Emotions* by Don Colbert, you will notice something unnatural about holding resentment toward others, that spiritual and physical bodies cannot bear. That is why the Bible warns us in Proverbs 4:23, to keep our hearts with all diligence for out of it are the issues of life. Interestingly enough, Colbert shares insights on how resentment, bitterness, unforgiveness, and self-hatred are toxic emotions that trigger autoimmune disorders, rheumatoid arthritis, lupus, and multiple sclerosis—proving the dangers of unrepented hearts, and the desperate need for genuine repentance in repairing one's body from toxins that inhibit health.

How does unforgiveness cause physical diseases? Although it may sound extreme, notable sources like Johns Hopkins Medicine support the fact that chronic anger puts one's body into a fight-or-flight mode, which results in numerous changes in heart rate, blood pressure, and immune responses.[11] Furthermore, it increases the risks of depression, heart disease, diabetes, and other health conditions. On the other hand, forgiveness has been proven to calm stress levels, leading to improved health.

Karen Swartz, director of the Mood Disorders Adult Consultation Clinic at Johns Hopkins Hospital, supports an unpopular

---

11. Johns Hopkins Medicine, "Forgiveness: Your Health Depends on It," November 1, 2021.

opinion that believes forgiveness isn't just about saying the words but "An active process in which you make a conscious decision to let go of negative feelings whether the person deserves it or not." It's crucial to remember that forgiveness is a choice, just like love is a choice.

Choosing to have a healthy mind, spirit, and body are decisions that go a long way in life. While festering deadly emotions inside doesn't benefit anyone, not even the person you are mad at, it destroys you from the inside out and has a ripple effect on those around you. Everyone is looking up to us and the way that we respond to difficult seasons. The way we conduct ourselves and maintain our hearts can either positively influence and prepare future generations or corrupt them.

No matter how hard it is to follow through with continual forgiveness, we have to keep trying. Otherwise, we will sow bad seeds and reap bad harvests. What kind of testimony do you want to leave behind, as a Christian, for the children, family, and friends who look up to you?

FORGIVING WHAT THE WORLD SAYS YOU SHOULDN'T

The Devil understands that there is power in forgiveness, which is why he will go to any length to destroy your marriage. He knows that identifying unforgiveness in your life will bring freedom and blessings to future generations. Hence, the strong delusion the Devil creates causes people to believe falsehoods, such as preventing many from understanding the concept of forgiveness, especially forgiving infidelity.

Those who do not believe in forgiveness or struggle with forgiving withhold forgiveness because they do not believe the person who's hurt them has changed or will change. This is widely seen in secularism but, as we know, likes to find its way into the church when open doors allow it. While this is more closely aligned with a trust issue, I think it's safe to say it also embodies a heart issue. That issue is due to our sinful nature.

Those who do not yet walk with Christ have not grasped the understanding of the Savior. He alone has ultimately sealed our ability to forgive each other because He forgave us of our sins. We know that forgiveness is a must to enter into a sinless Heaven, but for the unrepentant soul, forgiving something of this magnitude seems unattainable. However, this will change once they encounter God of the impossible.

Although our unsaved loved ones may mean well by advising us against forgiveness or remaining married after infidelity, their lack of spiritual wisdom may be detrimental to our walk with Christ. We must remain mindful of our actions and strive to be a Proverbs 31 woman, which may sound easier said than done especially when we are so tempted to be a Proverbs 21 woman instead—a contentious wife who insists on being a difficult person for her husband to live with (Prov. 21:9-19).

I'm also guilty in this area. By giving ear and finding comfort in knowing that I had a ticking time bomb hanging over my husband's head. I would start arguments with my husband that were absolutely impossible for him to win. Sometimes it would get so heated that he would beg the question: "Are you ever going to forgive me like you said you would? Should we really be married if you can't move past this?" Those questions hurt like a slap to the face, but they also forced me to think about my choices and challenged me to live more Christ-like. Another great reminder I had to live like Jesus is worship music like Cory Asbury's song Sparrows, "A heart that's planted in forgiveness doesn't dwell in the past."

That was when I finally realized that my best wasn't enough. I needed to totally surrender myself to God again and stop opening doors of resentment. I did not want to deal with the root issue at hand. Since I was the one wronged, I genuinely felt like mourning was okay. However, the way I was behaving was not mourning; it was a grudge that was forming. I was reminded yet again of what the lady from church told me at the altar when praying for forgiveness, "Are you truly ready to forgive your husband?" I felt dumb and weak for forgetting her subtle warning. Thankfully, God's mercy is fresh every morning, and I was able to grab hold of His throne when even my greatest efforts failed me.

Forgiving what the world says you shouldn't is such a hard thing to do; especially because we are such emotionally driven beings. Over time I have come to observe that the secular world has a hard time grasping this biblical concept: we reap more than we sow (Matt. 13:23). Therefore, it is literally to our benefit that we forgive our spouses daily so we can accept the good things God has in store for our futures.

If what we want most is for our marriages and families to remain together, find healing, and be fruitful, then we need to stop blocking the road to recovery. Without forgiveness, our marriages are doomed—and you don't have to be divorced to experience that. Just because someone chooses to stay married doesn't mean that they have put in the work to improve the relationship. It takes surrenderance, forgiveness, and hope that can only be found in Jesus Christ to pursue the will of God.

Otherwise, you both will grow into an old bitter couple whose marriage is still hanging on by a thread when it didn't have to end that way. Not only do we reap more than we sow, but we also reap later than we sow. As we see in Galatians 6:9, planting seeds in the ground is a great analogy to compare our marriages. Although they differ in the amount of time it takes to reap the harvest (the seeds of life have no timetable), the idea that a proper time is appointed for a harvest to come remains true.

OUR HOPE

Thankfully, Romans chapter eight offers hope for those who find themselves struggling to forgive. One day, God will restore our marriages to the way He first designed them. As we watch Him unfold restoration in our lives, we should be encouraged by His goodness. Not only can we be encouraged by the great things the Lord has set out for us, but we can also find hope in the miracles God has done in marriages throughout the church.

In our church, the assistant pastor and his wife are a couple that my husband and I admire. Their testimony and exampleship set a high bar that even my backslidden husband longs to follow because the fruit their relationship yields are visibly tangible for all to see. Specifically, one part of their testimony is something that Corey and I often ponder on, and that is how they were able to have a blessed marriage after experiencing cheating. Not only that, but I am always challenged by their exampleship to refrain from holding onto things of the past because of how big I desire God's plans for us to be; something their fruits have inspired.

> "Do not remember the former things, nor consider the things of old. Behold, I will do a new thing, now it shall spring forth; shall you not know it? I will even make a road in the wilderness and rivers in the desert." (Isa. 43:18-19)

How God's hand has worked miracles in their lives always amazes us and stirs hope. Reflecting on the testimonies and transformation stories of other's lives is the reason why I have chosen to stop allowing bitterness to eat me alive, replay scenes of the past, and open doors for Satan to have a foothold over my life. If He could restore them, there is hope for us, too.

Part 2

CHAPTER SIX

Vulnerability

Moving forward is the second most challenging part of this process because it requires trusting in God and allowing yourself to be vulnerable with your husband again. Previously, when I would spend time with my spouse and an old love song would come on, I was almost always tempted to switch the playlist because the lyrics transported me back to a pastime. I began to sink in and felt like our memories together were meaningless.

A time that I can recall this happening is when we took a shower together. The hot water began to steam up the air in the dark bathroom while a candle burned slowly, setting the tone as its copper dancing flames illuminated the walls. Corey would start our special playlist while we stood silently, soaking in the relaxing shower as the hot beads of stress washed off. Then, it would come on—the tunes of an old song that reminded me of our early memories together. I battled with accepting those moments we shared were unmatched by the ones he spent with her. Hearing our favorite love songs would instantly pierce the atmosphere and make me want to cry because I felt like those memories we associated with the songs meant nothing anymore.

But I had to, and still have to, remind myself how dangerously untrue those lies from Hell are and rebuke the Devil's snare. I fight my flesh daily by standing firm on God's truth and purpose for our marriage and locking in on my husband's face—in the now. In fact, being vulnerable has demanded that I focus on what is in the now and move forward.

On three occasions over the past two years, I have received four words from guest speakers who have prophetically spoken over my life, warning and encouraging me to keep moving forward and not look back into my past. Though each word was given throughout different seasons of our marriage, the one theme of never looking back remains true. That is because looking back at the past is a stumbling block.

Consider the parable of the pillar of salt. In Genesis, God reveals to Abraham that He will destroy Sodom and Gomorrah for their sins. Abraham then negotiates with the Lord to spare any righteous persons who live among the wicked in Sodom and Gomorrah. Then, angels warn Lot and his family to leave the city and *never* look back. However, in the midst of leaving, Lot's wife looks back at the city and is instantly turned into a pillar of salt (Gen. 19:24-29).

While this parable is frequently used as an example of what happens to somebody who chooses worldliness over godliness, it certainly demonstrates that no good thing comes from looking back.

The same concept applies to road safety; looking back while driving forward may cause an accident. Yes, we still look back from time to time when needed, but the idea is that when we're on the road, our focus is on what lies ahead, not behind. These truths have kept me grounded, and for the first time in my walk with God, obeying His will has kept me from returning to sin, as well as an unending hope and security in my marriage. Putting an end to looking back has opened the door to vulnerability in our relationship, allowing my husband and I to move forward.

Yes, you heard that right. We *both* work at not looking back because this affected each of us. Corey has to live with his past mistakes every day for the rest of his life just as much as I may be reminded of them. Corey made it apparent on various occasions that moving forward and not looking back was challenging for him, too, especially when I would fixate on his past mistakes. As mentioned at the beginning of our story, before I completely surrendered my hurt to Jesus, I made it a point to bring up his failures almost daily—such reminders interfered with his ability to be vulnerable with me.

We became vulnerable by God's grace and our emotional investment toward one another. The bonus is that the depth of our vulnerability has become more incredible than before, which is why every marriage should strive for vulnerability, keeping in mind that it is a continuous improvement.

THE BENEFITS OF BEING VULNERABLE

Some people see vulnerability as a threat. However, vulnerability plays an essential role in re-establishing a raw connection between you and your husband. If you're anything like me, you may likely find it difficult re-opening your heart to let your spouse see and experience you on a deeper level again, but it's *essential*. Vulnerability is one of the best parts of this restoration process.

That is because *now* is the opportunity to reconnect with your best friend after the violation. Yes, you have changed as a person since this has happened. You think differently. You process things differently. You are not who you once were, and now is the opportunity to share these new pieces of yourself with your spouse. Today is the day to put your faith into action and move forward because how can we expect to make things work if we refuse to put our hearts back into the hands of our spouses? Ponder these three ideas that can unlock hope for your marriage by being vulnerable:

Point 1: We must embody a willingness to reaccept the risk that comes from being open and willing to love and be loved again. Being vulnerable in this new stage of life after grief grants you courage, strength, and confidence, which are all Christ-like characteristics that God has gifted us during this season and beyond. We have come out stronger through this—and our husbands grow more inclined to develop a more profound love toward us because they have experienced the gifts of forgiveness and love. It's an opportunity to seek out your spouse and have discussions that will deepen your connection with one another.

For example, I asked my husband what his two main feelings were after I chose to remain married and still love him afterward. He responded, "I'm grateful most of all and relieved that my mistake didn't damage our marriage beyond repair." While I acknowledge that every person's story is unique, there is still a great takeaway. No matter how big the mistake, our spouses are still human beings with real remorse, like we are.

Point 2: God can take anything, no matter how broken or lost, restore it, and take it higher than before. That's the amazing thing about our Father. He is our hope not only for our sins but also for the sins of others. We should trust in the Lord during this season of vulnerability, where we are re-opening ourselves to rejection, triggers, and betrayal. We must exercise our faith in believing He is capable of restoring our relationships and watering the planted seeds in our husbands' hearts.

Watering the seeds of your husband's unsaved heart can be a battle. It takes fervent prayers and dedication to contend for their lives because the Devil wants so badly to destroy their souls. We must plant seeds of love as frequently as possible. Most importantly, we need to sow God's love—even when we don't feel like it (1 Cor. 13:4-7). We do this by demonstrating healthy habits, like sowing good words, actions, time, proper attitudes, and gifts of blessing into their lives.

Our unsaved spouses need us to lift them up with the words we speak; the tongue holds the power to honor our husbands or destroy them (Prov. 21:9). We are also called to sow seeds by giving our spouses physical affection, whether that be a peck on the cheek, a tender kiss that leads to a warm embrace, or regular intimacy. Similarly, spending time alone together is the best way to reconnect with a new love for your spouse. Aside from romance, trying to implement spiritual time together is essential. (In small increments, of course.) Or times of reflection that will build up your relationship.

Thankfully, my husband is open to lying next to me while listening to a sermon when we're traveling. This bond helps us reflect on our personal growth and marriage when given the opportunity, although this may not always work out for everyone. Another critical factor is to display a proper attitude toward him. When choosing to stay married, we must also be loving, patient, forgiving, and peaceful with our man. Lastly, we can water the seeds in our husband's hearts by giving meaningful gifts to them (Luke 6:38). What gift would bless your husband?

Through these good works, Christ establishes His throne and gives us favor as godly women and wives. As we contend for His calling over our lives, our husbands will take notice and see Christ through us. When our spouses take notice of the tangible evidence that Jesus is in our hearts—still loving him regardless of his past—they are more likely to feel emotionally accepted by us again (1 Pet. 4:8). I specifically see God softening my husband's heart when he begins to discuss private thoughts or emotions with me. At times, he will turn to me and share what he believes God is placing on his heart or something the Lord has shown him to deal with, which perfectly aligns with idea three.

Point 3: Our willingness to be vulnerable reopens the possibility for our spouses to be vulnerable back to us! If we can strive to recommit ourselves to this new reality, then there is hope for complete healing and total restoration in our marriages. What I mean by "recommitting ourselves to this new reality" is taking a leap of faith by no longer allowing past circumstances to stunt our marital growth in the present or future.

By coddling past hurts, you are standing in God's way and delaying your blessing. Though I recognize that healing and blessing can come from intentionally processing and addressing past hurts, it's crucial to avoid becoming glued to things of the past since we have no power over them anyway.

Allowing yourself to be overcome by a fear of the future limits your ability to reaccept the risk of loving and being loved again. When you are overcome with anxiety and doubt, reflect on Matthew 6:34, which warns us not to worry about the things of the future because tomorrow will worry about itself. Therefore, be vulnerable without worrying about things that are beyond your control. I cannot stress enough that I understand the fear, but it's unhealthy.

MOVING HINDRANCES

For almost two whole years, I was adamant about sharing our locations to hold each other accountable, and to an extent, this was necessary to establish healthy boundaries. However, with time, it became more of a fear issue. My mind always wanted to run and take my thoughts somewhere they didn't belong. After a year of my husband remaining faithful in our marriage, I could not let up about knowing his whereabouts. I tried so hard to control him out of fear of the what ifs, but it was only pushing him further away when what we needed was emotional intimacy.

One day, my husband went to do a side job with the assistant pastor of our church, whom he's known for years, and the topic of sharing our locations came up. The pastor goes on to explain to Corey that my having his location was a measure to make me feel in control, and if he were to have an affair again, Corey's decision would still be beyond my control—location or not. The pastor then strongly urged us to refrain from sharing our locations, hoping to rebuild trust more healthily. Ultimately, it came down to me. I needed to trust in God to find peace of mind.

Another ouch! It was not exactly the advice I expected, although it was the advice I needed. It was thought-provoking. My inner thoughts instantly became louder and louder, "Are we at that point already?" and "Am I willing to take that risk again?" So, of course, my stubborn self prayed about it, hoping for another solution that never came because the truth was, we were there, and it was time. The minute I accepted that I went into our phones and removed both shared locations—and never looked back.

Deciding to stop sharing our locations has been freeing. This vulnerable, necessary step helped me relax and become a better wife on the other side. I no longer need to check my phone every thirty minutes, worrying about his whereabouts. The stress of needing to know every step he takes no longer suffocates me. I began to feel more secure once I saw the boundaries we placed were something he was willing to pursue. As of 2025, I remain liberated from the griping fears that once held me captive, and our relationship still benefits immensely from this.

Letting go of fear allowed our relationship to flow more naturally. Corey would often initiate calls to inform me of certain plans that had changed for his day and sometimes text me during his downtime for a brief conversation. Watching him be considerate of my concerns and thoughts in life has been admirable and attractive. This shows that removing those barriers relinquished my vulnerability back to him and vice versa. That is an image of the Lord's unending grace. It brings freedom, peace, joy, love, and reconciliation.

THE SAVIOR'S EXAMPLE OF VULNERABILITY

Jesus demonstrates a perfect example of this, and if he did it, then that proves that vulnerability is good. In Matthew 26:37–39, we see how Jesus is honest with His disciples about how He felt during the most painful moments of His life. Not only did He share vulnerability with his friends, but He shared it with God and allowed Him into the depths of His emotions while wrestling in prayer.

Digging deeper into Scripture, we notice Isaiah's prophecy looks forward to one who will not break a bruised reed (Isa. 42:3). That is not because Jesus is a pushover or soft; it's because He knows how to apply strength to vulnerability. When you think about it, Jesus Christ readily made Himself vulnerable as a sacrifice for our sins on Earth. He knows what it is like to feel pain and betrayal in ways that are unimaginable in our lives. He came willingly open to receive bruises and lashes for our benefit. We can identify with Him during these times of fear and uncertainty. For that reason, we can trust that God will always bring justice to those who are wronged because He understands the battle in our minds and our difficult circumstances and is even more committed to our joy than we are. How wonderful it is to have a God who cares for us so much?

I love this revelation I came across while writing this chapter. The meaning of a bruised reed is immensely profound. It implies a deep contusion or an internal injury that's destroyed a vital organ. Here, Isaiah is alluding to a break you have beneath the surface that is crushing your spirit—that same injury has crushed the life out of your marriage and is hindering your healing process.

Very similar to love, vulnerability is a choice. When you choose vulnerability, you are not only accepting adverse risks that can potentially damage your marriage, but you are also accepting the positive consequences. What are the positive consequences? When we hear the term consequences, it is often associated with the negative connotations of someone's actions. However, there are also positive consequences for those who sow good actions. By sowing righteous actions, you are saying yes to receiving God's blessing for your marriage.

Corey and I have reaped great gifts in our unequally yoked marriage. By remaining open, honest, and emotionally available to each other, we are reaping the benefits of choosing vulnerability. Jesus is actively healing, restoring, and deepening our love for each other. I believe that is because of His promise in 1 Corinthians 7:14: "The unbelieving husband is made holy because of his wife . . . " These blessings in our marriage are tangible for each of us—despite spiritual differences.

Furthermore, we cannot sow seeds of fear or stress and expect to reap a peaceful marriage. Weeds like fear and anxiety are aggressive and hinder growth. So imagine the qualities you do want your marriage to have, and work backward by identifying what areas require you to sow different seeds.

We must sacrifice our fears and be vulnerable by communicating intimately with our spouses because it plants seeds that will return greater levels of intimacy. God's grace rewards acts of obedience, like loving your spouse brings great returns of love. Additionally, if we want to reap a beautiful marriage, we have to keep in mind that it begins with sowing seeds of love faithfully for a long time. Of course, this demands sacrifice from us, but our hope is that in God's perfect timing, we will reap good rewards, according to Galatians' proven law and process.

EMBRACING THE NEW

Lastly, intimacy demands vulnerability because sex is vulnerable. The reality is that our flesh innately tugs us toward insecurity—even more so after an affair. However, let us not be dismayed or afraid of making our bodies readily available to our husbands again. For a long time, I was worried and disengaged during intimacy because I was too focused on what he *might* be thinking. Over time, these fears and barriers began to dissolve as Corey and I engaged in sexual vulnerability. As he and I continued to show up as our most unprotected and authentic selves, our love-making was healing. Memories of the past began to fade away into an abyss of yesterday's problems, which freed us, mainly me, in our sex life. Another area that contributed to Corey's improvement was that every time we were intimate, he was fully present. He would ensure I felt special by sharing tender moments with me.

It involved embracing the fact that we didn't know how to continue with physical intimacy after the affair, but we contended anyway and were honest at times when we felt uncomfortable or incapable of moving forward. With time, we let go of trying to make love by how we thought it should look and began to allow intimacy to naturally unfold.

As we put our fears aside and accept that vulnerability is an essential component of marriage, we will start organically fostering closeness, intimacy, and trust. Without these things, our relationships become superficial, disconnected, and resentful, which is the complete opposite of what we're fighting for. This happens because fear disables our desire for intimacy. It causes us to put our guard up at all times, shutting down every opportunity for closeness with the one we love. When you decide not to be vulnerable in marriage, you are consciously choosing to hide your emotions and desires from your spouse. On top of that, fear scares us into demanding our partners to meet our every expectation—spoken and unspoken—instead of trusting God to meet them.

Since you've chosen to *stay*, work strongly at being intimately present. See your husband for who he is now, after experiencing your forgiveness, and not for his past mistakes (Heb. 8:12). We must remain willing to grow. To do so, we must be willing to meet others' deepest needs and protect each other's greatest vulnerability. As a result of sowing healthy seeds in your marriage, you will reap an environment of trust. Therefore, it allows each party to feel safe sharing more and develop a deeper bond.

My husband continues to show me he is committed to staying married by wanting to spend more time together, remaining open, and expressing his love by giving me physical affection on an ongoing basis, which is his love language.

Undoubtedly, our marriages will endure trials, but we must remember that although it may be difficult to be vulnerable again, it is still worth your effort, especially because taking risks with your spouse allows room for growth and connection within the relationship. For instance, an area of growth that needs to be explored once you've established vulnerability is trust, and I've got more on that next.

CHAPTER SEVEN

Restoring Trust

As mentioned in the previous chapter, we must sow good seeds in our marriages. Aside from vulnerability, another great seed to plant is trust. Without it, we can't expect it to grow. While there is no exact scripture that says God expects us to trust our spouses immediately after a betrayal—especially when regret and improvement are not immediately evident in our partner's life—we are still called to be patient and cautious with those who have offended us like Christ has demonstrated (Ps. 103:8, Prov. 14:15). We have to be mindful that in cases like ours, it may take more time and demand more effort from us.

Now, suppose your mate is repeatedly committing major offenses against you. In that case, you should confront it, lean on others and headship, set boundaries, and pause fully trusting him until you see evidence of genuine contrition (Matt. 18:15-17). Heeding this counsel is paramount to avoid overlooking his sins and holding him accountable for his actions. Doing so protects you and your marriage in the long run.

Something to consider before restoring trust: I chose to ignore his behavior in the first year of our marriage, which badly harmed us. When my husband was entertaining social media apps to talk to other women, I would try to remind him of our commitment to each other and explain the long-lasting effects of this sin. However, my failure to act when a boundary was crossed allowed this behavior to continue. Instead of being passive about repeat offenses, I should have stuck to my word by following through with consequences, such as physical separation, closing the door to all contact with other women, and proactive transparency with passwords.

Fear held me back from executing consequences for a long time, but calling out our spouse's sinful behavior (in love) and sticking to our word is crucial to seeing the change our marriages deserve. As long as boundaries are respected there is hope that trust can be restored. If we lack these things, we only fool ourselves into thinking that our marriages will improve. Yes, we are called to forgive, but we must also be wise and discerning. Ignoring and avoiding these boundaries will only do more harm than good. It wasn't until we were in the presence of two more believers and headship that my spouse became convicted of his actions and changed his behavior.

Aside from addressing the wise steps to take regarding trust after infidelity, before you can trust your husband, you must trust God. As a wife and mother who experienced an affair, gaslighting, and persistent bursts of anger, I can reassure you there is hope at the end of the tunnel.

SURRENDER EQUALS TRUST

God can and wants to restore the deepest pains of your heart if you'll only allow Him. I say this because trusting your husband means trusting in God. As we trust God during our trials, we must continue trusting Him when we get clouded by past darkness.

Let us not grow weary of doing good, for it is promised that in due season we will reap as long as we do not lose heart (Gal. 6:9). The Devil will try to get you to believe that the hope God is establishing within us and our marriages is too good to be true, but it isn't. Trust Him for all of your days, and He will take care of every need you have; spoken and unspoken. Though it's difficult to see past thick clouds, an infallible God sitting on the throne is entirely trustworthy despite our husband's errors and faults—and trust *should* be an expression of our faith.

God did not intend for us to trust our husband solely. His calling over our lives is much higher, and it involves trusting the Lord with all our hearts. By trusting He knows what He's doing, he will lead us onto a righteous path (Prov. 3:5-6). I was at fault in this area for such a long time, and the reason was that I idolized my husband. I didn't quite realize how heavily I relied on him to fulfill my needs until I started paying attention to all the nagging I did about his shortcomings. Whenever he failed to make me feel worthy, validated, or loved in the way I wanted him to, I set him up for failure because I was expecting Corey to play God.

Didn't I know that only Jesus could fill the void in my heart and meet my needs?

One of my most significant pain points was my need for affirmative affirmation. On top of the insecurity that came from our early marriage, I also struggled with the need to feel good enough all my life. This insecurity stemmed from daddy issues—also known as attachment trauma—that I had not yet completely let go of. I was unable to feel secure and required constant assurance because of this attachment issue in our relationship. Often, when I would seek out this affirmation from Corey, he would call it out and tell me that I needed to forgive my father for his absence during my youth and stop expecting him to meet those unrealistic needs in our marriage.

My unrealistic expectations of him were detrimental to our relationship and later required lots of healing to restore it. I am confident this heart issue was also a direct result of our marriage's foundation (fornication). The truth is, marrying my husband after fornicating did not fill these voids for me, just like it did not cure our lust—hence the affair. It's a heart issue that needs to be addressed at the root of the problem: our sinful nature. Getting married was like a band-aid solution. Although I am glad I married Corey, we both regret the rebellion our marriage was founded on because we see how damaging it has been on our lives.

It wasn't until I laid this idol down (my husband) and centered Christ as the King of my life that I found freedom and was finally able to proceed with restoring trust in my husband throughout our healing journey. I committed to this by acknowledging, confessing, and surrendering my idol to Jesus. I began striving to fill my mind and heart with Heavenly things and place the Lord in His rightful place. In doing so, Jesus gained total access to address any fears of my future. Scripture tells us that the things of tomorrow will worry about themselves, so focus on trusting God above all things to unleash His sovereignty in your circumstances (Prov. 23:17-18). Trusting Him does immeasurably more than worrying and unbelief does.

Once you've put your trust in God, you will embody a love that is long-suffering toward your spouse (1 Cor. 13:4). Without it, the progress in your marriage will continue to be hindered if you don't let go of what you *think* you know and instead try to learn from God by trusting Him. If you have or are currently deciding to commit to staying and making your marriage work, you need to do the work by exercising your faith and putting complete trust in Jesus. A piece of scripture that can bring direction during this season is Matthew 5:37, which urges us to follow through with our commitments, "let your yes be yes and your no be no."

Pursuing these acts emphasizes reconciliation. Through Jesus, we can take negative thoughts captive and re-establish trust after a betrayal. This truth became accessible while maintaining a deeper and more intentional prayer life. Striving to be in the Lord's presence as frequently as possible kept my mind at ease, making it more attainable to trust my spouse afterward without being regularly mentally attacked. Jesus's first sermon challenged people to change their minds, which tells us two things: it is our responsibility to take control of our thought lives, and He makes it available for us to do so (Prov. 4:23, Matt. 4:17).

NO JESUS, NO JOY

With that said, not investing enough time in our relationship with God results in fear, anxiety, intrusive thoughts, and anger. Lack of trust prevents us from moving forward and stunts the growth of our marriage. Specifically, it reduces our level of commitment, intimacy, and the sustainability of our relationship, which may increase the risk of divorce. Statistics show that 58% of couples who discussed the situation that caused the lack of trust were able to rebuild trust.[12] Proving that trust is a key factor in reconciling a damaged relationship.

I noticed I was more prone to distrusting Corey when I was inconsistent with my prayer life. Even after he tried so hard to prove his commitment to our relationship, I struggled to believe that he was trustworthy and would make him jump through hoops to regain it, which was unfair treatment for him. It was like my lack of prayer affected the condition of my heart, which influenced my ability to forgive, hindering trust. It was a domino effect, and when I caught this revelation, I made it a point to stay consistent with my prayer life and surrender all hindrances to God. My prayerfulness allowed Him to work in my heart and restore trust in my marriage.

As Christian's, faith translates into action, and in this case, it needs to begin with our trust in God so our spouses can be in a position to earn our trust back. It is 100% worth it when we are faithful to our commitment to rebuild trust with our spouse until the end. Choosing to remain married should mean that your yes means yes, so you take one step closer to re-establishing a deeper connection between you and them. Although trust won't rebuild itself overnight, we can be encouraged by Scripture: 1 Corinthians 13:4. Let us persevere by praying for the strength and patience that rebuilding trust demands so that we can reap the benefits of forgiveness and long-suffering love.

---

12. Natalie Maximets, "Can a Marriage Survive without Trust: Online Divorce," January 29, 2024.

ADDRESSING THE FORMER AND REMEMBERING THE LATTER

Many relationships strained by infidelity can overcome this new reality by humbly addressing the former (2 Cor. 2:11) and happily remembering the latter (Jer. 29:11). This is so we can remain peaceful and build ever-stronger bonds. The first time I heard this idea, God dealt with me and inspired a word for this chapter. Specifically, He clarified that if we want to move forward after betrayal, we must address what has already happened and the promises that lie ahead. By gracefully reflecting on what your marriage has endured and believing in the future God has for us, we can find rest and restore our relationships.

When we choose to remain married after infidelity, we are making an informed decision about continuing our lives with the person who has hurt us. Therefore, it is our responsibility not to get stuck in the past. The blood shed for our sins is the answer to all things. Jesus's blood gives us the power to overcome fear and resurrect our dead trust in our husbands. Coming to grips with this new reality by accepting the damage done while keeping in mind God's goodness in store for us is critical. Let us understand that this marital suffering does not limit our hope for our future with our husbands.

Another thing to consider regarding the former and the latter is what the Bible says about those who are poor in spirit (Matt. 5:3). This involves an honest evaluation of ourselves and a deep understanding that we are all sinners who have violated God's trust, just as we have experienced in our circumstances. The former is Adam and Eve in the Garden of Eden. They, too, betrayed God, but He still clothed them amid their sin and sent His only Son, Jesus Christ, as a living sacrifice to overcome the power of death. The good news is that we can trust the Lord's unwavering faithfulness, and he will restore trust on our behalf.

In Proverbs 3:5-6, Solomon expands on this idea by stressing the advantage of trusting in God instead of relying on our understanding. Remember, He specializes in restoring brokenness. The

Lord wants to see us through this trial, but our lack of faith often restricts His access to move on our behalf. Find confidence that He will strengthen you and teach you to trust your husbands again instead of leaving you in despair.

Our ability to rebuild trust with our spouses stems from our unwavering confidence in our Savior. Believing He will never fail us sets the foundation for trusting our husbands again. Our ultimate security is only found in Jesus, giving us the freedom to trust our spouses and experience the joy that comes with it.

OUR DUTY AND HIS PROMISE

As Christians, we have a duty to reconcile with one another. Outside of marriage, that may not always result in remaining friends with someone who has broken your trust. I am confident that in marriage, a part of reconciling with our husbands demands us to be a ministry of reconciliation, as seen in 2 Corinthians 5:18. Since the Lord sent Christ to Earth to die for our sins and restore His relationship with humanity, that should, again, remind us of its importance. That hope is made readily available to us. We must reflect the Lord's glory in our marriage by believing our husband can change. As long as we pray for His guidance to pursue our duty in reconciling our marriage, He will faithfully answer our prayers by helping us overcome this challenging, necessary step.

Our hope in rebuilding trust in our marriage lies in the fact that our God can do *anything*. Even though trusting your spouse might seem impossible, I pray that you stay encouraged and know that His promises for your life will come to fruition.

Trusting in the Lord is the most critical factor in how your marriage will recover from the affair. He will restore and fill in any gaps that separate you from the marriage He wants for your lives. Yes, there will be times when you might get frustrated with yourself and fall short of trusting your husband, but don't stop there. Keep in mind that rebuilding trust is a journey, never a destination. If you hope your spouse will meet a standard of perfection, you will be disappointed. Place your hope in Jesus; He will meet your every need and desire.

In that light, re-establishing trust allows goofiness and quirkiness to resurface in our relationships in hopes of rekindling romance with each other. And what greater joy is there than God fulfilling His promises over our lives? I encourage you to evaluate your heart during this season. Is lack of trust hindering growth in your relationship? If so, pray over yourself; that fear's grip will lose its hold on you, in Jesus's name, so you can enter into the goodness our Heavenly Father has in store for you and bring your marriage to new heights.

CHAPTER EIGHT
Rekindling Romance

What key components can we draw from the concept of rekindling romance from how God demonstrated love toward us? In John 13:34, we see that God desired to restore man to Himself through love because it is through love that He was compelled to send His only Son to reconcile man to Himself. This truth reveals that He's deeply invested in love and marriages and cares profoundly about reviving relationships. So, if our marriage is of significance to Him, then a counterpart of that is rekindling the romance—or intimacy—in our marriages. Remember, no matter what your marriage has been through, love has the power to restore a broken, wounded relationship just as man was restored to God through love.

HEALTHY AFFECTIONS

After repenting from unforgiveness and choosing to forgive your spouse daily, it's time to reconnect. This process should look a lot like re-establishing trust. By maintaining a healthy relationship with God, you will be filled with healthy affections that will channel into your relationship. I've found that my affection for my husband grows when I pray and read my Bible every morning, listen to sermons during the day, and stay encouraged by songs of praise. How can that be? God is love; embracing Christ is embracing Christ-like qualities that spark an affection for your significant other.

Since my husband does not walk with Jesus, the steps he takes to channel affection into our relationship don't necessarily involve any spiritual aspect but are healthy nonetheless. For example, he prioritizes sex and physical touch frequently, takes on responsibility, enjoys quality time together, and is sensitive to my needs. These forms of affection draw us closer together and help keep the flame of romance alive.

Whether you have children or not, spending quality time with your spouse should be a priority. Specifically, we should work intentionally to make a continual effort to spend time with them regularly. It can look like going on date nights together or simply curling up on the couch while chatting about their day. In my world, spending quality time together as a family looks like this:

Our black 3500 Dodge Dually is parked under the largest tree in our cul-de-sac. Corey typically uses his downtime to clean his work truck, gather his welding leads, clean up trash, organize his tools, etc. Although cleaning a vehicle is not usually associated with romance, when your spouse's love language is quality time, you will find that your presence is all they need to feel affection from you.

Most of the time, I am not naturally inclined to go outside—especially when the Texas heat is blazing hot—but when he takes the time to stop what he's doing, check on me, and ask me to join him in the yard, I can't refuse. Why would I want to deny him quality time and affection at the expense of my comfort?

Declining would be selfish. I imagine all relationships experience moments like these, when they have an opportunity to draw close or stay where they are comfortable. (This may sound extreme, but if you think about it, you'll find it true.) As small a decision as this may seem, in moments like these, we can build our marriage or stunt its growth.

While I sit at my desk and write, and my husband reminds me he's waiting for me and would love to have me outside, my eyes are drawn to the door as I blush over his desire for me. So, I closed my laptop and decided to join him outside. While I open the front door to exit the house, I see my daughter kneeling beside Corey, handing him his tools; already, I have zero regrets. Seeing her face light up and her eyes fixated on me, yelling, "Mommy, look!" while helping her father is priceless.

Why would I want to stay inside?

Corey looks up and smiles as I unfold the chair he left available for me—that image is priceless, too. Although I'm often comfortable staying inside with the A/C, I can see that it not only pleases him that our daughter helps him or plays near him, but my company also pleases him. Again, taking the time to be present with your spouse speaks volumes to them, especially if one of their love languages is quality time. Now, that's not to say that these efforts will mean less if your spouse has a different love language—in fact, you should make an effort to find out what their exact love languages are—instead, it's about being mindful of each other's emotional needs.

For two years now, I've made it a point to quiz ourselves on our love languages. I normally don't give my attention or time to quizzes that test personalities since things like the Enneagram Personality Test are on the rise. Side note: I caution against this because it holds unbiblical principles. Please be prayerful and discerning of the spirits (Heb. 5:14). However, I love Gary Chapman's 5 Love Languages Quiz because it helps you discover your primary and secondary love languages, what they mean, and how to implement them in your relationships.

In the first year, we took this quiz, my primary love language was acts of service, and my secondary was words of affirmation. Corey's primary was physical touch, and his secondary was quality time. Fast forward one year, and our love languages shifted. I suppose these changes occur when individuals are in a different season of life. I say that because I found it interesting that our love languages exchanged places. My new primary love language was physical touch, and Corey's was acts of service. Weird, right?

When I considered this, I reflected on this life-changing event's impact on both of us. It proved to me that after the affair, our priorities shifted. Corey put my needs before him by demonstrating acts of service, and I put his needs before mine by practicing physical touch. Each of our choices had an unintentional yet striking effect on our romantic chemistry. What I'm getting at is that taking baby steps toward caring about what your husband likes and investing the time to learn his love language is the beginning of feeling more connected to each other.

RECONNECTING

There is a profoundness in the micro-moments of love despite how social media and advertising portray romanticism. Although traveling to Europe or receiving a shiny, expensive gift from your spouse may sound like a dream, it is truly the seemingly meaningless moments that are the most meaningful connections. Acts like tenderly touching each other when you walk by go a long way. You can either miss out on the opportunity or seize the moment to turn toward your partner and build trust, emotional connection, and a passionate sex life.

While exercising these things is easier said than done, the hard work you deposit into your relationship will build toward getting to know your spouse. As quality time increases, you will begin to notice new opportunities to tap into your husband's heart. Believe me, falling back in love with your man is such an emotional rush (more on that in the next chapter). Building upon the romantic chemistry you both share is an incredible journey to go on as you revisit all the reasons why you fell in love with him in the first place.

This looks like exchanging questions that will help you understand each other at a deeper level. As simple as it may sound, anyone has the potential to yield great results when they ask questions, remember answers, and ask more questions. The key is to be intentional. Admittedly, I believe you never stop learning about your spouse. It's especially crucial to get to know your husband after the affair to see how this experience has changed them and even yourself.

As mentioned earlier, retaking the 5 Love Languages Quiz gave us insightful ideas to consider. We already knew that we were changing for the better of our relationship because we could tell by our actions, but when we discovered how it had changed us, we grew encouraged. We were encouraged that the good seeds we had sown were now noticeable. We were reaping the fruit of our hard work.

Do you know their new hopes and aspirations? What are their current worries and stresses? Take advantage of time alone to dig deep and bond. If you find yourself struggling to form questions, get the ball rolling by using Google to get the creative juices flowing. Taking those first steps by taking that gear stick out of neutral and putting it into drive will take you on a new adventure with them! Remember that the more thought-provoking the question is, the larger the emotional investment both of you make.

For instance, I love asking questions about my husband's upbringing. Growing up, he had a rough life. So when we talk about his childhood, it reveals parts of him I've never seen before. I also love exchanging self-reflective questions that help us see what areas we have grown in or maybe are stunted. These thought-provoking questions build trust and a greater bond between us as we relate and exchange compassion for one another.

Since our marriage bond matured, we have grown to appreciate each other more deeply than before. Corey and I are individually different, almost unrecognizable, from what we looked like in the first year of our marriage. Personally, I've noticed that I've grown in areas of trust, patience, peace, joy, forgiveness, gratitude, and love. For Corey, he has demonstrated growth in areas of love, commitment, empathy, forgiveness, contentment, slowness to anger, self-control, and accountability.

I think it's safe to say our marriage would have starved to death if these changes never occurred. After the affair, we realized that neither of us was genuinely meeting love's expectations to have a long-lasting and impenetrable marriage. We understood there needed to be change. I couldn't expect my needs to be met if I wasn't meeting my husband's, and vice versa.

Pastor Aaron Campbell describes this idea perfectly in his book *Love's Expectations*. He shares this insight about his first wife (deceased) and his second wife, "I did not expect to receive anything from them that I was unwilling to give. That is the beauty of love's expectations—there is a mutual desire for each party to fulfill each other's needs."[13]

Realizing we are both new people after the affair has urged us to get to know each other for who we are *now*. This revelation made me realize how great He is. He truly made man in His image, even to the point where our marriages are to mirror His relationship with man. Our marriages are alive like Christ and are designed to be cared for and watered daily. Otherwise, they shrivel up and die.

Our relationship with Christ is no different. If we stop reading His word to get to know Him, we lose sight of who He is and our *desire* to be in the word. Likewise, our marriages demand that we get to know each other and keep getting to know each other so we can continue having and sharing healthy affections with our lovers.

Another parallel God has shown me (that relates to Him and marriage) is that we become more like Him when we spend more time in His presence. Similarly, it's been proven that the longer you are married to your spouse, the more you become alike. How neat is that? These truths confirm God's desire for us to embrace closeness, put effort into our love life, and our need to dedicate time toward rekindling romance!

THE SUBMISSIVE WIFE

I know you probably read the word "submissive" and immediately scratched your head, questioning, *how is that romantic?*—but hear

---

13. Aaron Campbell, *Love's Expectations*, 17.

me out. If you really want to take this romance thing to a new level, it's worth evaluating your submissiveness radar. You can start by honestly considering these questions:

- Do you willingly submit to your spouse as an act of obedience to Christ?
- Do you respect your husband's point of view, or at all, for that matter?
- Are you slow to anger, speak, and maintain peaceful communication?
- Are you supportive of your husband's emotional, physical, and spiritual needs?
- Do you complete household chores while he plays his role of providing financially?

Ephesians 5:22-24 demonstrates that a woman who is determined to honor God will, in return, willingly submit to her spouse. Now, this does not mean wives are inferior or should be oppressed; it is about biblical order. An anointed preacher and author named Voddie Baucham explained this perfectly in a sermon entitled *Love and Marriage: The Better Half* (watch via YouTube). This sermon breaks down key elements related to a biblically submissive wife that I think is worth noting—especially for those who may find it difficult to respect their husbands.

Pastor Baucham discusses the fall of mankind in Genesis 1-3 by placing emphasis on Genesis 3:17.[14] He explains how Adam was held accountable for sin entering the world because he failed to exercise his God-ordained dominion over Eve. In Romans 5:12, Paul says, "Therefore, just as through one man sin entered the world, and death through sin, and thus death spread to all men, because all sinned." Baucham points out that the scripture doesn't say "through one couple," and that is because Adam had headship over Eve. He continues:

---

14. Voddie Baucham, "Love and Marriage: The Better Half," January 15, 2013.

> "The problem with the fall was an issue of order. Before the fall, God created man, and He gave the man the woman, and the man and the woman are to have authority over the beast: God, man, woman, and everything they had dominion over. But what happened in the fall was that the beast deceived the woman, exercising dominion over her, then the woman tempts the man, thus exercising dominion over him, then the man eats [of the fruit] in order that he might be like God. They flipped the order upside down; that's the fall."

The Bible clearly demonstrates to us that a biblically submissive wife is required; otherwise, there will be consequences. For those wondering, yes, this applies to unequally yoked marriages, too. As long as our spouses are not asking us to sin, we are still called to submit to their authority as head of household. So, when we submit ourselves as the weaker vessel to our husband, we are not only obeying the Lord, but we are blessing our spouse.

Living by this is crucial, especially when healing a relationship after infidelity, because we naturally revert to pride and bitterness, holding us back from submission. Intercession: If you find yourselves relating to Eve, these words are not meant to discourage your efforts or condemn you. They are to awaken your purpose as a woman of God so that you can be fruitful in achieving a stronger bond with your husband. Should you feel conviction for not pursuing God's will in this area, I encourage you to repent and ask Him to help you become submissive, as well as a Proverbs 31 woman.

Since order is so important to God, we can only imagine how important He has made it in the hearts of our spouses. Even if a man is not saved, I think it is evident that our submission as a woman is indispensable to him. Confidently following our husband's lead and supporting his leadership is an attractive attribute men crave from their wives. Hence, submitting ourselves to our husbands as an act of obedience to God strengthens the marital bond.

Submission places us right where we are called to be as godly women and ignites a flame in our husband's hearts. That is why I placed this subject in this chapter specifically because it wasn't until I heard Baucham's sermon months after discovering the affair that this truth resonated with me and served as a lifeline for my marriage. When I intentionally implemented this godly wisdom, I discovered submission releases passion, excitement, and attraction.

Submission was one of the last precursors that contributed to the restoration of romance for my marriage—which we desperately needed then and will continue to need as life goes on.

Since I have a Bachelor's Degree in English, I do my best to utilize my talent and education by maintaining a clientele and juggling various projects that come and go, whether that be writing or editing projects. At the same time, I am also a stay-at-home wife and mom. Truth be told, those roles and responsibilities clash frequently. I am often conflicted because working from home while teaching my daughter life skills and raising her takes away from my work schedule. Let's just say I'm working on mastering a work-life balance!

While I love what I do as a creative, being a wife and mother is my highest calling, second only to being a follower of Christ. Therefore, the pressing need to execute my household duties in a timely manner (not rushing to complete them before Corey comes home or neglecting them altogether) is nothing short of being a submissive wife. I put my family and household duties above my career primarily because doing so demonstrates honor to my husband and reciprocates his appreciation for all he does as our family provider.

I won't lie and say I have this down to a T 24/7. However, after increasingly being confronted by Corey about my need to prioritize household tasks above my career, submitting to his reasonable requests to maintain our home has only yielded positive results, making loving each other easier. Without that submission, we are prone to arguments, nagging, and friction, leading to division in our relationship. Failing to submit is just not worth it.

What *is* worth my time is waking up earlier and staying on schedule. That way, I can complete my household duties with ample time for my projects and have time to spend with my family once Corey gets home. Choosing to avoid laziness and procrastination may not sound like a form of submissiveness for a wife, but it sure is. You might see a noticeable difference in your husband's demeanor right away! As long as you strive for consistency, in Jesus's name, a breakthrough will meet you halfway.

Since we've discussed how healthy affections, reconnection, and becoming a submissive wife can steer our hearts in the right direction toward rekindling romance, we'll now discuss how to put romance into action.

ROMANCE IN ACTION

After almost half a year of holding onto a gift card given to us by my dad and stepmother, Corey and I had finally decided to make some time alone (*without* our kid!). I'm not sure why it took us so long, but we certainly wished we would have prioritized that alone time sooner. (I'll take a shot in the dark and assume that you too may need to prioritize this in your season of life.)

That evening, I wore a dark green dress that had hung in my closet for over a year—also ridiculous. It was a hammy down from my aunt that also came with a matching pink dress, but not just any hammy down; these were brand new with the tags still on them. A year later, I still felt blessed to have them. Anyway, I wore the green one since Corey argued it complimented my hazel eyes better.

Of course, I got dolled up, and he wore his nice black button-up with dark blue jeans and his new Ariat boots. We both looked our best and were ready to go. During the whole twenty-minute drive downtown, we held hands with the windows rolled down. I sensed I was not the only one who felt relief. Once we arrived downtown at our destination and got inside to our table, the atmosphere grew a bit awkward: How did we not have anything to talk about? Had we really run out of things to say only two and a half years into marriage? Our situation seemed momentarily tragic.

After pushing through the awkwardness and small talk, we finally made headway and started laughing and joking with each other. When our date was coming to an end, we didn't want it to be over yet, so we took our date to the truck and talked some more, but this conversation went deeper. I was pleased that we pushed through the temporary moments of struggle, bringing each of us to the depths of our hearts—we didn't want superficial.

Eight months later, our date nights became more fun, relaxed, and natural. For example, last night, we had a date at Olive Garden. We parked, exited the truck, and made our way inside. The wait time was about ten to fifteen minutes, so we sat on a bench outside together while we waited for them to buzz our phone and tell us our table was ready.

The atmosphere between us was flirty and joyous. We chatted for a few minutes as our stomachs growled. Then Corey grabbed my face and kissed me while chuckling, trying to lighten the mood before saying, "Let's go to Mama's and get nachos instead!" His efforts to sway me into agreeing were applaudable, and I almost caved but didn't want to drive the distance. We debated about leaving Olive Garden to find a fast-food restaurant nearby, but then we chose to stay put.

About six minutes later, we received the text that it was our turn to be seated. We scurried inside and ordered our food before ordering the drinks—you would think we were starved. We split a Chicken Tortellini Alfredo and the endless soup and salad dishes. Right away, I asked Corey two questions that I knew would catch his interest, "How much money do we need to save this year to purchase land? And what type of investments do we want to get involved with to generate passive income?"

His eyes lit up and traced the walls, "Around thirty thousand dollars. And instead of jumping into container homes next year, let's invest in a multi-service industry shop first. Something that offers a barbershop, nail salon, and lash extensions all in one." I thought, "Well, that got his attention!" and carried on with our conversation by asking more questions.

At first glance, when we sat down, we were already blankly staring at each other, and I could sense an awkward moment trying to ensnare us. However, I pushed the pedal to the metal and used some brain power to show my interest in growing and becoming successful together. So yes, even eight months later, we sometimes found ourselves pushing through stuffy moments. However, we bounce back quickly when we put an effort into rekindling romance. This is romance in action: effort!

Imagine if I had allowed fear to dictate our date in that brief moment when it seemed like we had nothing to talk about. If I had fixated on that fear, my inner thoughts would have imploded all over the table like a random, nasty barf. Face your fears head-on and ditch the miserable attitude. I guarantee you both that you won't be sorry and will always feel rewarded for putting in effort.

Although romance may not come naturally as it once did, contending through uncomfortable moments like these when you feel like your efforts are fake or insincere is worthwhile. I say that because we cannot expect every sacrifice and offering to *feel* good. In fact, feeling uncomfortable is a sign of growth, so embrace it!

It felt so nice to regain that spark that had been diffused for some time. The first date I mentioned was a turning point for us. After that, we both agreed to spend more time going on dates alone. Since then, our relationship has been more at peace. We are able to step out of our regular day-to-day routine and just enjoy one another's company without responsibilities.

Our continuous effort to pursue one another is paying off greatly. I can't help but compare our romantic growth to a recent event we shared during Christmas and through the New Year of 2025. For Christmas Eve, we hosted a small gathering at our home, and late that evening, a couple of the menfolk worked to get the fire burning. It was quite a challenge to get the wood to burn since it was rained on a few days prior. When the damp wood proved difficult to light, the group made a tipi with logs and poured canola oil into paper towels after they ran out of lighter fluid.

With their determination, innovation, and patience, they created a strong fire. While we all sat together, Corey continued to add more logs and poke around in the pit. At first, I thought it was silly he spent so much time messing around with it. Later, I understood that it was his continuous pokes that maximized the airflow and its ability to burn the wood, causing the fire to burn on until the next week. This fire got me thinking about how similar my marriage is to it.

The more we poked at the fire and added wood, the higher the flames burned and the deeper the heat entered into the ground (so much so that the ground around the pit began to sink a bit). Likewise, rekindling the romance in a dead marriage serves as oxygen that keeps the fire burning strong between a couple. Without the efforts to inject romance into your marriage, it will eventually die. So don't let the flame of romance become cold ash—keep poking to keep it alive!

HEALING SEXUAL HURT

For months after the discovery, we also experienced awkwardness in bed together. For a while, it caused conflict and strained our sex life, but we chose to stay locked in and fight the turbulence head-on, which later improved our sexual intimacy. There were times when insecurity or intrusive thoughts about his affair would overrule me, turning me off and causing me to be less present and hopeful for a good evening together, which influenced his mood to become impatient and frustrated by my lack of effort.

Then, at the end of the night, we'd both be immensely frustrated and discouraged, handling it the wrong way by turning our backs to each other without even saying goodnight. Ouch! Is that you? Moments like these hurt. They make you feel like a failure and sink into yourself because you feel miles away from your lover when, in reality, you are only inches apart.

Though they were difficult moments to get by, allowing time for our frustration to subside was a good idea, but we did it with the wrong heart and attitude. It wasn't until many months later that we began to grow more patient and understanding of one another. So if, and when, a dilemma did arise in the bedroom, Corey would reassure me that it was okay, he wasn't mad, and that we could try again tomorrow—and we would.

Honestly, his positive attitude, patience, and understanding began to initiate peaceful outcomes on nights like these. I, however, was fixated on self-pity and insecurity for a bit longer until Jesus helped me release those sexual hurts and move forward. Nevertheless, when your spouse is not at the forefront of your mind when you are trying to make love, it is best to try again later (whether that same night or the next morning) but with a good attitude. You never want to go to sleep angry and vexed because it only brings turmoil. Being patient and understanding only worked out for us 100% when I was reciprocating and accepting Corey's calmness and positivity.

If I had continued to doubt him even after he tried to diffuse the situation, it could have resulted in an argument or frustration, like many times before. That is because instead of trusting that he meant every word he said, I let fear grip me, cause me to worry, and become contentious. Not only did my fear begin to hinder us from rekindling romance, but I also allowed unwanted triggers to dictate my feelings and actions toward him.

It is not wise to allow yourself to go to this place or remain there. The Bible says in Proverbs 17:28, "Even fools are thought wise if they keep silent, and discerning if they hold their tongues." That tells me that my unsaved husband was doing his best to exercise wisdom while I did the opposite. Instead, I challenged him and struggled to accept a good thing he was trying to do: take a timeout and retry when both our heads were in a better place. Reflecting on this now, I see how my negative attitudes and wallowing were silly and counterproductive; I wish I had recognized that sooner rather than later.

The point is to *never* stop trying. If Corey and I had given up on restoring sexual intimacy, our marriage probably would have failed. Why? If I had stopped trying to be intimate with him, it would have strained our marriage even more. Then, the Devil would have used it as an open door to creep back into our lives. I'm grateful that is not the case. Since sexual issues often mirror marital issues, find confidence in this: as your relationship heals, your sex life will, too. By the grace of God, I can testify that a sexually hurt marriage *can* be healed because it's happened to us. Not only that, but our bond during intimacy is *greater* than in previous years.

My prayer for you is to never let low self-esteem or selfishness hinder you. I pray you never give up on your sex life and always be patient, kind, forgiving, and understanding of one another. I pray this because once your sex life is dead in marriage, your relationship with your spouse will soon follow. The truth is, when you invest your time and focus on rekindling romance and intimacy, it brings honor to your spouse and strengthens your marriage. Strive to take initiative and be patient no matter how weird or frustrating it may feel at first, and you will be glad you did!

Lastly, when you pray for your marriage, rebuke the spirit of division and ask God to help you reconnect with each other on a deep level, become a biblically submissive wife, and restore where you and your husband have been sexually hurting. Remember, He has the power to redeem your marriage and take it to new heights like never before.

CHAPTER NINE

Letting Love in Again

After feeling lost in the dark for so long, the light at the end of the tunnel seemed far away. To some, this may sound dramatic, but the trials of the first year of our marriage felt never-ending. We were drowning in despair, and total reconciliation appeared intimidating, as if it were too good to be true until Christ intervened and reassured us that there was still hope for our marriage.

Maybe that is where you and your spouse are today: intimidated by the darkness suffocating your relationship, left feeling hopeless. If so, allow me to share 1 Peter 1:22-23 and 1 Peter 3:8 as friendly reminders that fervently loving each other overlooks a lot of flaws, making that "light at the end of the tunnel" way closer than we think. In that, any relationship, no matter what trials it has endured, can find freedom and love again through Jesus.

LOVE YOUR HUSBAND GOD'S WAY

Loving your husband as Christ loves you involves letting go of attitudes that hinder love. It demands that you and I respect them in the same way we expect to be treated (Eph. 5:33). Thinking back, I can see where we made mistakes, which triggered us to build walls against each other to protect our hearts. For Corey, that was day one of our honeymoon.

As briefly mentioned in the first chapter, an old boyfriend of mine named EJ had died tragically during a hit-and-run about four years before marrying my husband. When Corey and me reconnected, the depression from EJ's death was still slowly falling off me since I had returned to Christ two years before. Still, the thought of his death was something I struggled to bounce back from.

During our honeymoon, we drove to South Padre Island and passed EJ's burial site near his hometown, Harlingen. As I stared out the window, recalling all my memories around the town, Corey noticed a familiar sadness that shadowed me. Honestly, the sudden change in mood was not something he could ignore since we had just been peacefully laughing and joy-cruising moments earlier.

As he watched my extreme excitement fade, he asked what was wrong. I shared with him the tradition I had made for myself: to stop by EJ's memorial stone when my travels brought me back to the area. My beating around the bush was clear. I implied that I wanted to take time from our honeymoon to visit his grave.

My implication was a major blow to my husband because not even 24 hours after saying "I do," I put another man before him in a seemingly innocent attempt to voice my feelings on our honeymoon! Was that loving my husband God's way? At the time, I was trying to understand what was wrong with what I said because my feelings were valid, right? Wrong.

Putting another man before my husband, especially as a newlywed, was insensitive and demeaning. Looking back, I understand how this seemingly innocent moment of expressing my feelings was thoughtless, directly triggering Corey's self-defense mechanism. To be clear, Corey and I had already discussed my feelings about EJ and the depression God was saving me from, so the level of trust was there to freely express how I felt, but it was not right of me to expect him to take me to do that then. It was the wrong time and the wrong place to initiate that conversation.

This poor decision on my end provoked Corey to withdraw almost immediately. That night, when we arrived at our destination, he grew emotionally callous and took a big step back in our relationship. After talking with my husband the other night about this event, he admitted that my desire to prioritize EJ played a big role in his wall-building toward me.

My actions demonstrated the opposite of love; they expressed indifference. Honestly, this is a word I don't use in my vocabulary regularly, partially because I thought "hate" was the only term for love's opposite. Nevertheless, I find the word "indifference" most appropriate here to convey how attitudes influence actions. Below are two definitions for indifference from the Cambridge Dictionary and Oxford Languages:

1. "Lack of interest in someone or something."
   —Cambridge Dictionary

2. "Lack of interest, concern, or empathy."
   —Oxford Languages

Although these definitions differ slightly, I chose them because they each have something to offer my story. Cambridge's definition of indifference best suits the example above. I understand why Corey felt I lacked interest in him and our special day; I was thinking of another man. To him, I'm sure he felt he couldn't compete with someone whom I previously loved and had died.

Oxford's definition includes "lack of concern" and "lack of empathy." Quite frankly, expecting to make a pit stop on this particular road trip for this specific person was self-seeking and inconsiderate. Not only did I appear to lack interest in Corey and our honeymoon, but I also lacked empathy toward him and was not concerned about how something like that would make him feel—which should have been at the forefront of my mind.

So there you have it. My indifference toward Corey and our honeymoon gravely distressed him, fanning the flames of twenty-two years of rejection he battled with. The indifference he felt from me came with major disadvantages, such as emotional walls, isolation, and poor decisions that followed shortly after this, leading up to the affair. When we slack on loving our spouses in the way God intends, we rob ourselves of all that love has to offer.

I would like to quickly pause and mention that the purpose of including this story is by no means an excuse for my husband's mistakes. Rather, my goal in using this example is to deepen your understanding and provide awareness on why loving our spouses God's way is the best way to begin falling back in love and remaining in love with them, as Christ is helping me.

Romans 3:23 gives us a great piece of wisdom to reflect on: we are all imperfect people who have sinned and fallen short of God's glory. Meaning that we, too, have sinned against our husbands. Maybe in different ways and at different levels, but sin nonetheless. And as you read the example above, you probably noticed that my indifference toward Corey was a form of sin. Here is a quote from David Bowden's book, *Rewire Your Heart: Replace Your Desire for Sin With Desire for God*, that captures the issue of sin perfectly:[15]

> "You sin because your affections for the gospel are weak, while your affections for your own provision are strong."

Each of us made selfish decisions. Loving each other our way instead of God's way kept us at arm's length. Though we occasionally had good days, we mainly allowed how we treated each other to become dependent on our happiness or mood. When that happened or our love became one-sided or conditional, we hid behind the walls we had built. But God calls us to do better than that. He desires for us to love our husband as He loves us, which is unconditionally and sacrificially (John 15:12).

With that in mind, we see how the Devil exploits our sins to bring division between us, especially in the deepest ways, like love and marriage. So how can a couple fall back in love after a holy covenant is defiled?

While metaphors make it sound like falling in love is something easy to do (like accidentally tripping over a step), it is actually

---

15. David Bowden, *Rewire Your Heart: Replace Your Desire for Sin with Desire for God*, 42.

more deliberate than that. It will take work, as you have noticed in the previous chapters. Again, *allowing* yourself to fall in love with your spouse is even more intentional because God challenges us to love them in the same way Christ loves us. Although it is no easy task to *always* love your spouse in the same way God loves us (particularly when our selfishness inclines us to sin, whether intentional or not), it is possible (1 Cor. 10:13).

Identifying when these initial letdowns took root is helpful for anyone who wants to move forward and fall back in love with their spouse again. That's because if we lack accountability for our actions and choose to remain ignorant of the source of the problem, the leaky faucet will never be fixed. Yes, we can ignore it as long as we want, but that doesn't change the fact that you have a broken pipe somewhere! In fact, neglecting the problem results in more damage and bigger headaches, which is true in many other aspects.

Likewise, it is key to identify the source of your negative attitudes. Doing so will save you and your spouse from years of unnecessary heartache and pain. Hence, it is a time-sensitive situation: identifying and uprooting unresolved resentment, hindering us from loving our spouses unconditionally. The benefits of purifying our hearts are clear. Our love for our significant other grows, allowing us to support them through their internal barriers while drawing us closer to a Christ-like love.

This is where staying married becomes truly liberating because loving your husband God's way brings freedom and joy. It is interesting to think about how God wants to use your life to reflect His unconditional love for your unsaved spouse. I'm eternally grateful for being a part of such an experience—what an honor it is! Every marriage deserves to experience what we are actively a part of: God providing us strength to contend for our marriage, softening our hearts to each other, and showing us how to love one another more deeply than before.

LOVING WHO HE IS IN THE PRESENT

My husband and toddler were cuddled beside me in bed one night. Corey had just finished a twelve-hour shift, and Aria had no naps that day. We were pooped. First, Corey began drifting to sleep, then Aria followed. Me? I was barely hanging on, running my fingers through Corey's hair, when a thought took my mind.

As I tilted my head to the right and traced Corey's peaceful face with my eyes, I couldn't help but feel an overwhelming sense of gratitude. My mind took a mile-long run in a matter of seconds as I glanced at him and then at them. It was an unexpected moment when I felt immensely grateful to be his wife. I lay there in awe, caressing his head, amazed by the man he grew into.

I kept trying to wrap my head around God's goodness. But His faithfulness to me, my family, and my marriage is inexplicable. I had no words to speak, only tears of joy. All I could do was thank Jesus for answering my prayers. There was so much reverence for Him in that moment as I pondered the growth, restoration, and healing He had done for us thus far. What's even more fascinating is knowing God is not finished writing our story, and there are more marvelous plans to come.

An image of Corey like this years earlier seemed unlikely. Never in my wildest dreams could I see us coming out of those dark moments ten times stronger than before. Yes, I knew God was capable of anything, which was a major reason for holding on, but I could never see us enjoying our marriage down the road. Our living happily together and being reconciled seemed so far away. Many times, we'd question out loud or privately to ourselves whether that day would ever arrive. But thank God that moment snuck up on us and reminded me that night that I have so much to be grateful for—and so do you.

We didn't arrive here overnight. This process took intentional effort and was only possible if we were willing to accept change and fight for each other. I had a major problem that prevented me from loving Corey. I needed to stop expecting him to be someone he wasn't.

Since I had such high hopes for his *potential*, I could never love him for who he was because I was so focused on who he could be. Not that there's anything wrong with encouraging your significant other to grow, but it can easily become unhealthy if we lose appreciation for the person they are in the present. I struggled to accept Corey's flaws and opinions because they did not align with my beliefs. Day and night, I would find myself nagging at him over his bad habits. I was constantly bothered because I could not find joy where he found joy, and vice versa. It especially hurt at times when he would go outside to drink or smoke. I felt insignificant.

Although I knew he had good intentions by not asking me to go outside with him when he engaged in those activities, I couldn't overcome the feeling of rejection. I thought he was choosing himself over our family, making us the least important. However, I now understand that this is not the case (within reason) because there is a bigger issue that only Jesus can resolve: the sin factor. In hindsight, I acknowledge I was doing my best to live a clean and holy lifestyle, but holding him to the same standards I lived by was unfair.

I had a self-righteous attitude that was suffocating him. Honestly, my arrogance was extremely off-putting to Corey and alienated me from him, damaging our marriage. As a Christian wife, it wasn't my job to badger him or remind him where his sin was taking him. My job was, and is, to demonstrate the love of Christ through my words and actions, which my dad gently reminded me of often. After I accepted this and asked God to show me how to love Corey in a Christ-like way, He helped me see past our differences.

This is the wonderful discovery behind loving my husband for who he is today—not who he used to be, nor who I think he can be after experiencing the gift of salvation—and what has brought substantial growth to our relationship.

Although it took me a while to grasp this understanding, I'm grateful for these teachable moments. Though relationship experts may encourage couples to remember all the reasons they fell in love in the first place, I can confidently attest that this alone is not a sustainable way to rebuild a marriage. I stand by choosing to love your husband for who he is in the *present* every day because it gives the Potter access to shaping your love for one another in His hands.

Another problem after the affair was I lacked love for Corey. This part is for those who have "lost" or "fallen out of love" even the slightest. While I believe love is not always a feeling and that it is a choice, I also understand the immense pain brought on by this crisis punctures holes in our hearts that seep out the love we carry for them.

In retrospect, not everyone experiences this loss of love for a spouse; some may question why they still love a man who cheated on them. But oftentimes, others feel like they are falling out of love because they find it too hard to be close their spouse again. Whether they admit it aloud or not. They know all too well what lies within their hearts—no matter how hard they try to hide it.

I encourage anyone who is struggling with these mixed emotions to confront them because nothing kills a marriage more poisonously and silently than bitterness and lack of love. When this happens, it is almost like we must learn how to love them again after the affair. Growing in love for your spouse again is something God will train you to do through the Holy Spirit over time. Trust that when His love enters a home through one person, it restores life, infecting it entirely with its contagiousness. God's love is far-reaching, irresistible, and has the power to revive love in the dead places of your marriage.

The point is, sometimes, we need to honestly evaluate our hearts to see if lack of love hinders us from loving them freely. Should that be you, consider that your actions determine if love lives on or ends. Since love is a choice, here are some practical steps I work at daily that anyone can implement, too, when striving to love their spouse:

- Avoid competing agendas
- Pray for them daily
- Less nagging and more respect

- Find unity through differences
- Live with grace
- Prioritize your relationship
- Show your love (learn their love language)

As long as each partner is willing to respect the other and work to grow together, I am confident there is hope for the unequally yoked. Don't believe me? Take a stab at it yourself for at least six months straight and watch the change that will unfold.

CONTENTMENT DURING RESTORATION

When Corey was ready to put in the work necessary to rebuild our relationship, I found myself in a place of discontent. How unfair was it that after all the pain he had put me through, now he was finally ready to make things right? My mind was focused on how unhappy I was and never on what I had to be grateful for, which fueled arguments and frustration. Who would have known that one little piece of discontent can spiral into resentment and bitterness? Still, God wanted to restore me, my husband, and our marriage.

In dictionary terms, restoration means returning something to its original state. However, biblically, the word restoration has greater connotations that surpass the everyday usage most are familiar with. In Scripture, the Lord blesses those for their faith and hardships by giving them back what they lost, and sometimes more. The idea is that God wants to refine you, your husband, and your marriage beyond measure!

Let's expand on the restoration concept by looking at David's testimony. In 2 Samuel, we see that he dramatically fell from God's grace at the beginning of his reign as king. After committing adultery with Bathsheba, the wife of Uriah the Hittite, she became pregnant, and he had Uriah murdered to keep their infidelity a secret. These events brought David to a place of repentance, leading up to the well-known prayer found in Psalm (one of my favorite worship songs, I might add).

> "Create in me a clean heart, O God, and renew a steadfast spirit within me. Do not cast me away from Your presence, and do not take Your Holy Spirit from me. Restore to me the joy of Your salvation, and uphold me by Your generous Spirit." (Ps. 51:10-12)

Though these verses are about David's yearning to be restored to God, the concept of restoration still offers a beautiful promise to believers in broken marriages. It proposes that restoration can be applied to God restoring the joy we should have for our marriages since it is a sacred covenant between God and a couple.

Just as David is a model of restoration, any marriage can model restoration after a betrayal. Christian or not, marriage is a sacred covenant between God and a couple, and God wants to make our love for our spouse and marriage stronger than before the affair. He cares about us in ways we don't even think to care about ourselves. That is something Corey and I could have never done alone; only the Father in Heaven can do such miracles. Besides, He doesn't only want your marriage to survive; He wants it to thrive, and nothing is impossible with God (Luke 1:37).

According to Gitnux's Market Data Report on Marriage After Infidelity Statistics, "77% of couples report having a stronger marriage after recovering from infidelity."[16] To be clear, I am not suggesting that anyone should be content with infidelity because it's important to see consistent, trustworthy behavior over time. I am suggesting that after your spouse has demonstrated his commitment repeatedly, it is possible to love him at a deeper level than before.

Even though this study wasn't conducted on unequally yoked couples specifically, the thought of 77% of couples thriving after healing from adultery is amazing. How much more would that percentage increase if, at least, one partner followed Christ? The possibilities for our marriages are endless if we learn to be satisfied with what God has already done.

---

16. Jannik Lindner, "Marriage after Infidelity Statistics," June 23, 2024.

Scripture instructs us on how to work toward contentment in our relationships, in this case, our marriages. For that reason, cracking your Bible open to read and study daily is essential for growing in our understanding of the word and becoming increasingly conformed to God's will. Reading the Bible helps us discover how God wants us to apply contentment in our marriages during the season of restoration.

> "Now godliness with contentment is great gain."
> (1 Tim. 6:6)
>
> "I am not saying this because I am in need, for I have learned to be content whatever the circumstances." (Phil. 4:11, NIV)

Learning to be content during restoration is important because it enables us to accept our husband's and marital circumstances with peace of mind. Think about it. When someone is discontent, they are usually miserable, which makes their spouses miserable, too. They have difficulty finding happiness and are never satisfied with what they have, always expecting and demanding more. As I reflect on my previous shortcomings in loving Corey for who he is rather than who I wanted him to be, it is clear that my discontentment was driving a wedge in our marriage.

Discontentment is like a distraction. The Devil uses it to lure us away from being happy in our marriage and tempts us to long for what we don't have and resent where we are. This device is easy to use when we're angry or resentful about things that have gone wrong in our marriage because we already feel robbed that our spouse didn't meet our expectations or uphold their vow. When you think about it, husbands grow discontent toward their wives *before* infidelity. What does that tell us? If we allow discontent to have a foothold over our minds, without Jesus, it won't be long until our bitterness opens the door to poor decisions.

For instance, being discontent made me feel hopeless. I started becoming so unhappy in the marriage that it led to negative feelings toward Corey. Not long after, bitterness hindered me from loving him fully. It became so unbearable that I frequently fantasized about ending the marriage after an argument occurred. I am pleased that I never followed through with those temporary moments of rage because then I would miss out on the joy and restored love we share today.

If you are up for an adventure, falling back in love with your spouse is an exhilarating experience. Also, if you find it difficult to *feel* like you are in love with him right now, even though you know the love is there, don't be ashamed; be patient with yourself. Keep choosing to love him daily, and you both will find yourselves in a new, unconditional love for one another with profound appreciation.

A HUSBAND'S LOVE: WITNESSING A MIRACLE

As I wrote the final chapters of this book, I turned to Corey for his perspective on choosing to love me daily after everything. I thought it would be special to include his personal experiences that might speak on behalf of other husbands on their way to healing. What he said was interesting because his experience highlighted a theme many couples in my fellowship and outside our fellowship have experienced during restoration.

His words were, "I loved you more after the affair."

Granted, my husband's experience might differ from the next, but I think the data I provided on the percentage of thriving marriages suggests the same thing Corey admitted. Husbands are not only capable of loving their spouse more than they did before, but there is a high chance many will! It makes you wonder why divorce blogs don't discuss these odds, huh?

I suggest this happens because the unfaithful partner understands their decisions could have wrecked their lives and those around them, causing them to develop a deeper appreciation for their spouse when they choose to stay. Corey said this: "When you decided to stay married to me after everything, there was no more doubt about your love for me, and then my love for you grew." Although Corey never personally knew what being in love looked like, the Christ-like love I demonstrated through forgiveness and choosing to be with him daily exemplified that. We all have different experiences that shape our lives; these are the ones that have shaped ours.

Letting love in is something the unfaithful person also has to choose to do. When they do it, it reverberates into their spouse's life, creating a more perfect, long-lasting union. Imagine missing out on a miracle like that if you walked away, even if your husband was genuinely willing to change. The book of Jeremiah 29 contains a powerful lesson about choosing to stay.

In it, the prophet Jeremiah wrote a letter to the exiled Israelites living in Babylon. If you take the historical context of his letter, it is safe to suggest that many people might have thought a man of spiritual stature would certainly be calling them to battle. To gather together, rise, and fight their way back to the Promised Land. Wrong. His letter surprisingly calls them to do the exact opposite.

God dealt with Jeremiah to tell those who had been exiled to stay—like He knew they would be blessed for remaining still despite the external forces that were working against them in the present. Instead of calling His people to leave, God calls them to stay because "if [the land they are in] prospers, [they] too will prosper" (Jer. 29:7, NIV). Similarly, the Lord may be calling you to stay because if your husband spiritually prospers, you will prosper.

As wives, it is possible for us to feel like an exile after the affair. Maybe you feel disconnected and alone or fear being rejected by your husband again, so you pull away and are now exiled from him. Whatever the case for you, I am sure the thought of packing your bags and "claiming the goodness of God's promises elsewhere" has been tempting, but is that what the Lord is calling *you* to do?

Understanding this parallel between the exiled Israelites and exiled wives can change our lives if we yield to the voice of God. Choosing to stay and letting love in again may mean you will witness a miracle in due season. We must stay tuned to God because it helps us remain attentive to what He is doing and what choices He wants us to make in our lives.

CHAPTER TEN

Allowing Yourself to Be Transformed

"And do not be conformed to this world, but be transformed by the renewing of your mind, that you may prove what is that good and acceptable and perfect will of God."

—ROMANS *12:2*

"Slowness to change usually means fear of the new."

—PHILLIP CROSBY

It is scary doing something you have never had to do before. When Jesus came to Earth knowing that He would have to sacrifice His life in order for us to have a chance at making Heaven our home, I am sure He was afraid of dying and what the future held (Matt. 27:46). Think about it: no one else had lived a sinless life nor died innocently on the cross to pardon the sins of humanity. Yes, Jesus knew coming to Earth and dying for our sins is what His

Father called Him to do, but that doesn't mean following through with God's will came easy to Him.

Jesus still had to suffer indescribable pain physically, spiritually, and emotionally—to the point where He sweat blood—as part of His sacrifice. Like any human, He was scared and hoped to be spared the pain if it could be avoided. Did Jesus think *every* person He would die for, born and unborn, would repent and enter into Heaven? No, He knew what the odds were and what was at stake. As described in Matthew 7:13-14, the gate to Heaven is called "narrow" and the gate to Hell is called "wide." In other words, the amount of people who choose to reject Jesus and the gift of salvation will be greater than those who will accept Him into their lives as Lord and Savior. Still, He mercifully died for us anyway, *knowing* that many would betray Him and choose eternal death over eternal life.

If Jesus would have let fear dictate His decisions, Heaven would not be an option for any of us today because no sacrifice would mean no hope for the human race. Despite the trials and uncertainty His future faced, He still carried out His Father's business. Through His obedience, God carried Him through the shadow of death. Resulting in a miraculous resurrection, more personal miracles, His ascension, and taking His seat at the right hand of the Father. By the same token, we can also share in that confidence that God will carry us through our valley, even though we may be afraid, weak, and hurting.

It is innate for every human to fear change during this time, because our futures are unknown. However, when fear overrules our minds and causes us to make choices based on comfort instead of submitting to the will of God, we can be led astray. When fear leads to resistance, resistance can lead to thoughts of quitting or unintentionally self-sabotaging our relationship. In return, our lack of surrendering impedes the transformation process He desperately desires us to have both personally and maritally. In other words, our resistance to change prevents us from experiencing total healing.

It is never enough to be healed only halfway. Think of your situation as an open wound that became infected. Common sense tells us it wouldn't be enough to only take antibiotics in order to have it heal properly, right? You would also need stitches to help the skin come together again because stitches support and strengthen wounds, minimizing risks of bleeding and infection. Likewise, when we allow God to transform us, those fears of the unknown are mitigated and we are strengthened to move forward and contend for a healthy marriage.

I return to the sacrifice Jesus made. Through Scripture, we find it was only through His obedience that God was able to carry Him through the fear of dying and death itself. Not only that, but Jesus gained victory through His resurrection. If He had allowed fear to take over then He wouldn't have discovered the reward of obedience and surrendering to God. Imagine what awaits *you* after the pain of this affair, if staying married is His will for your life.

Remember, we serve a mighty God who is capable of anything.

A great verse to refer to during this time of uncertainty is Psalm 23:4. I suggest this scripture because I love David's vulnerability in admitting there is real evil around him to be afraid of. I admire how he doesn't belittle the darkness he is up against nor submit to fear. Instead, we find him thanking God for being connected to him, leading him as a Shepherd, and comforting him. What a powerful awareness he had to pray this during such a dark time. Thankfully, this same shepherd and comforter makes Himself readily available to us. We only need to allow Him total access to our hearts in order to be transformed.

THE BRIDE AND GROOM

Our Savior understands what it is like to step into the unknown after betrayal. He understands our fears about being married to the same person who has wronged us, because as His bride, we have wronged Him too. Take a look at how Jesus's "betrothal promise" during Passover is His bride's (our) guarantee to Heaven and how He understands our pain of betrayal like no other.

In Jewish times it was tradition for a prospective husband and his father to travel to the woman's house and have dinner with her and her father with special offerings. After agreeing on a price for her dowry, the young man's father would pass his son a cup of wine, known as the Cup of Blessing, which he would then offer to the lady to seal a betrothal covenant. In other words, when the son is offering his prospective wife a cup of wine, he is signaling to her that he is giving his life to her and is asking for her hand in marriage. By drinking the cup, she displays her consent to enter into marriage with him, promising him that she also gives her life and agrees to the marriage.

During Passover when Christ is telling His disciples "This cup *is* the new covenant in My blood, which is shed for you," what He is really saying is, "I love you all. I am giving you my life, will you give me yours as well and marry me?" Jesus relates to our suffering because He has suffered too, by our doing! Still, despite the endless betrayals we put Him through, His love and commitment to us is unwavering. Though we were caught off guard by the betrayal, God was not; and He still desires for us to keep our covenant as He has done for us.

THE POWER OF CHANGE

Are you hopeful, or want to become hopeful, for a better future with your spouse, but fear of letting go is hindering the transformation God has set out for you? If you answered yes, I get it—fear is intense and intimidating. Choosing to stay married under these circumstances is surely uncertain and unpredictable. Even more so, the futures of our marriage can seem increasingly scary after looking at others who have shared in our heartache and resulted in failed marriages.

Despite the lost hope worldly and some Christian marriages have on display, what is the key to overcoming fear of the unknown when choosing to stay? It is to allow God to do His perfect work in your life by sanctifying you and strengthening your marriage. Only by surrendering your all to Him will you be set free from emotional bondage. Ultimately, how you choose to respond to sexual betrayal reveals where your faith stands and what you believe about the Lord.

Maybe you once believed sexual betrayal was an unforgivable act, impossible to forget and reconcile, but now Jesus has given you hope and wants to change your mind. Although it might not feel like it, God wants to use this trial to build you spiritually by growing your faith. The Devil understands that if the Holy Spirit heals your mind that it will teach you to help your husband find freedom, too. Hence, his determination in creating crafty lies that will stir up fear to impede you from God's blessings.

Our Father is in the business of changing minds and wants to change yours today about choosing to stay in your covenant. He has the ability to remove self-focused and secular mindsets that work against your efforts to reconcile your relationship. He is the God of transformation who is perfect in all of His ways. Letting Him renew your mind gives Him access to change the way you think about choosing to stay, which will change your inner character and life into His image.

In *The Supernatural Power of a Transformed Mind*, Pastor Bill Johnson states, "You know your mind is renewed when the impossible looks logical . . . to see negative situations reversed for the glory of God."[17] That, my friend, is the power of change. And when our perspective of reality changes, the way we view and handle the affair will change. By accepting and applying this truth, Christ can transform your broken marriage into one that glorifies Him.

CLAY IN THE HANDS OF THE POTTER

Letting the Lord reshape a broken marriage you have spent months, or years, on trying to fix yourself is difficult. It is like everything in you wants to take control and do what the flesh tells you to—leave or harbor unforgiveness. However, when the world is screaming "You deserve better" and "Move on" at us, we have to choose to

---

17. Bill Johnson, *The Supernatural Power of a Transformed Mind: Access to a Life of Miracles Expanded Edition*, 2016.

let go of our fleshly desires and allow God to be the Potter of our lives. Being transformed is a process that invites you to surrender to God's unseen plans for your life.

> "And the vessel he was making of clay was spoiled in the Potter's hand, and he reworked it into another vessel, as it seemed good to the Potter to do. Then the word of the Lord came to me: "O house of Israel, can I not do with you as this Potter has done? declares the Lord." (Jer. 18:4-5, ESV)

We desperately need God's tender hand to remold us and give our marriages another chance, even if choosing to forgive and remain married does not come naturally. One story in the Bible that demonstrates reconciliation after infidelity is found in the book of Hosea. I highly recommend reading chapters one to three to understand Hosea's story in its entirety. Specifically, chapter three provides valuable insights on how God instructed Hosea to remain married despite his wife's repeated adultery:

> "And the Lord said to me, "Go again, love a woman who is loved by another man and is an adulteress . . . " So I bought her for fifteen shekels of silver and a homer and a lethech of barley. And I said to her, "You must dwell as mine for many days. You shall not play the whore, or belong to another man; so will I also be to you." (Hos. 3:1-3, ESV)

Some lessons we can learn and apply from Hosea's hardships is that God molded him through his obedience—he submitted to a call of faithfulness. While Hosea may not have understood God's assignment, he obeyed anyway. Not only did his obedience in keeping his covenant represent God's unfailing faithfulness to Israel, but I believe He was also molding and preparing Hosea for something greater *after* the betrayals.

Additionally, the Lord used Gomer to personify the actions of the Israelites who kept betraying God by worshiping idols, while using Hosea to personify Himself through faithfulness. Thankfully, God affirms to us, through Gomer's life, that no one is beyond forgiveness and restoration. Although God's purpose for their marriage was beautifully complex, it demonstrates the standard that He wants us to follow; which is to love as He loves us.

There is endless mystery within the Lord's plans for our lives, but one thing that remains certain is His love for us and His desire to restore our brokenness. Whether that be the brokenness within us or our marriage, He wants to remold us into something beautiful. His promise to us today mirrors that of the Israelites then. God can, and will, restore our marriage under a new covenant as he did for Hosea and Gomer.

When sexual betrayal causes a marriage to appear dark, hopeless, and defeated, God is just getting started. How amazing is a hope like this? It makes me awe in wonder how magnificent the God of all the universe is. To illustrate what I mean, I would like to share a revelation God used Corey to deliver to me.

After our Sunday evening service, my husband, daughter, and I went to Mama Margies for dinner. On the way there Corey and I were talking about the new tint he put on the truck. Fearing the tint was a little too dark, I kept suggesting he roll the windows down since the sun was gone. As we arrived at the restaurant Corey positioned the truck to reverse park—a laughable obsession he has. While he did that, I didn't make a sound, yet he took notice of the fear in my eyes because he knew I couldn't see anything (accredited to my poor vision).

He chuckled at my fright, continued parking, and relaxedly said, "Don't ask me how I can see it, just know that I do." Moments later, we stepped out of the vehicle and his parking was perfect! How Corey could see what he was doing when I could barely see out of the window beside me puzzled me. Was I experiencing a physical analogy related to trusting God?

Before you close the book and say I am over analyzing, hear me out! Although Corey's remark may sound lighthearted, I immediately felt God speak to me at that moment. It was an eye opening experience that encouraged and confirmed what He wants every hurt wife to know about choosing to stay after betrayal. That is to stop worrying and questioning *how* He sees hope for us during dark times and simply *trust* Him when He says it is possible.

Allowing the Potter to mold me has, and will be, an ongoing process that requires surrenderance. I cannot, and would not want to, imagine a life without my husband and am eternally grateful that Christ has made a way for us to find freedom in choosing to stay together. Throughout this process He has granted me the courage needed to step into faith for Corey, which is blessing our union like never before; and He wants to do the same for you.

PATIENCE DURING REFINEMENT

"What then am I to do once I've gotten this far?" A question you may be asking yourself, especially if you have already implemented these practical, Christ-centered tools. The answer to that is simple, yet tedious—be patient. Yes, I said what I said. In order for us to reap the benefits of choosing to stay we have to allow God time to refine us, our husband's, and our marriage.

When the healing for your marriage seems slow, refer to 2 Peter 3:8, "But, beloved, do not forget this one thing, that with the Lord one day is as a thousand years, and a thousand years as one day." Hopefully in doing this you will find understanding that even miracles have their place in God's timeline. He is not in a hurry and there is no rushing Him. Keep in mind that God is after deep restoration in us and His focus is on eternity.

Every couple and their situation is unique, so the duration of refinement will depend on your relationship's intricacy. There is no real telling the exact moment your marriage will begin reaping the goodness you have sowed, but it certainly is worth the wait. It could be as soon as six months, or up to two years. Regardless, God needs room to do what He does best—restoration.

So take time with your spouse, slow down, read your Bible, and embrace what is at work before you. Ask the Lord to show you when and how to pause and slow your heart and soul. I guarantee you and your husband will benefit from this. Be encouraged:

> "The Lord is not slow in keeping his promise, as some understand slowness. Instead he is patient with you, not wanting anyone to perish, but everyone to come to repentance." (2 Pet. 3:9, NIV)

Another thing to consider about the slowness of your marital restoration is it may be a nuance of God's grace at work. If that is the case you can find confidence in Jesus that your husband is being dealt with and learning about the causes of the offense. One could say patience during this time is a form of long suffering (Cor. 13:4). There is immense value in this virtue, which you can study about in Galatians 5:22.

The word of God promises us in Colossians 1:11 that He will, "[Strengthen us] with all might, according to His glorious power, for all patience and longsuffering with joy." In this season of waiting, consider this long suffering as a gift from God that never allows us to give up hope in the improvement of our marriage.

It is our duty as Christian wives to realize relationships are not disposable. Especially among Millenials, Gen Z, and the latter, who are known for a disposable culture or being a throw-away society. Relationships are not objects! They can't just be tossed out when they get damaged or because you *feel* it no longer serves you. There is a high cost for people who treat their marriages as disposable; they miss out on experiencing a lasting love.

You've seen it before, whether you paid attention or not. I know Corey and I see it everywhere we go. That lasting love is found in older couples. They have something we all want, but don't want to work for. Their life transitions throughout the decades have deepened their love for each other in ways young couples might not, yet, understand. Provided this lasting love is only shaped by lived experiences.

Over the ages they have shared positive experiences, like having children, buying a home, or starting a business. All of which are happy, memorable milestones to reach together. Yet, many seem to ignore or overlook the fact that they have shared in heartache also. They could have also shared negative experiences, like outliving a child, going bankrupt, or battled with an affair. I'll be the first to admit it is easy to want something beautifully rare, but not want to sacrifice what it takes to have it.

Nevertheless, if we want a love that lasts we have to accept that enduring hardships is inevitable. Marriage may not be easy, but it is worth fighting tooth and nail for. If you desire the deeply gratifying and joyful marriage older couples have, you have to be willing to go through the refiners fire to get there. It is only through the fire that we are refined and made strong. Unfortunately, joy doesn't give us that—hardships do.

In August of 2024, Corey and I saw a tiny cute older couple in Farmington, Missouri at a Huddle House. They looked our way, we looked toward theirs. While they waited for their meal, at one point, I noticed the husband scoot so close to his wife that their arms were squished together. The wife fanned him off and slid over a little, shaking her head, snickering at him. She said something to him that I didn't hear, as though suggesting he was being too silly. Then her husband whispered something in her ear, grinning happily.

While paying great attention to the details of their feisty and playful interaction, I wondered what all they had been through to get them there. Then their fun-loving attitude reminded me of how far my marriage has come because often we imitate that same quirkiness in our everyday lives. Seeing them made me hopeful and inspired. Now, writing this, I also wonder, who will we influence if we allow ourselves and marriages to be refined?

PURPOSE FOR PAIN

Forgiving infidelity is an act of courage and a stepping stone to freedom that changes who you are and influences those around you (Eph. 2:10). We've talked about how when our circumstances don't make sense, we can still find hope in Jesus who helps give us purpose for our pain. What's more is this: You can use your painful experiences, and the lessons you learned, to help liberate others. You know God wants to use your pain to bring you closer to Him, but do you know that He wants to use your testimony to bring others close to Him, too?

When we share our experiences and how the Lord has helped us, we show others the light that is God living in us. Although you might not go as far as to consider yourself an expert in the field of forgiveness, if you have progressed in your healing journey you are further along than another hurt wife. Thus, you are a suitable conduit to understand another person's pain, fear, and confusion. You can be that somebody in their life who prays for them and they can confide in and cry on your shoulder.

Who knows who else they have to depend on during this season; some have nobody. Most are too ashamed, or too prideful, to admit they need help or prayer. It is no coincidence when you feel the Lord pressing upon your heart to talk to somebody you don't know about something so personal. His selection is not random. He is the God of personal miracles and wants to save others from unforgiveness and broken marriages, but we must be obedient to the call.

> "For you have been called to live in freedom, my brothers and sisters. But don't use your freedom to satisfy your sinful nature. Instead, use your freedom to serve one another in love." (Gal. 5:13, NLT)

It may be hard to picture you are serving others by sharing your testimony of betrayal, but imagine how your experiences can lead someone else to freedom. What is good for the Father is good for ordinary people, like you and I. We just need to let Him use us as vessels as a part of the grand plan. Your story can bring hope to somebody's dark circumstances and be a light that leads their marriage to restoration. It is better to be uncomfortable for a few minutes to possibly lead someone's marriage to Jesus, than to remain silent as their marriage crumbles.

Within the last few years I have had the opportunity to witness, encourage, and pray for other women, some believers and others not, who have been sexually betrayed by their spouse.

I always try to put myself in their shoes and consider what they must be going through. More often than not, I have noticed that they choose to initiate the end of the marriage. Sometimes I find myself reflecting on the potential of each couple and praying that forgiveness is brought to the forefront of their minds.

Of course, I do recognize there are instances where reconciliation is not an option. Should that apply to you, I pray you do not feel shame or condemnation for ending the union. Jesus loves you regardless of your marital status and wants you to know you are precious in His sight. He will never abandon or forsake you. Though at the end of the day, everyone has free will and cannot make choices for their partners. As long as you remember forgiveness is still necessary for total healing from this trauma, Christ will carry you through.

NEW FUTURE: JOY, PEACE, AND HOPE RESTORED

Adultery has a way of stealing joy from us, but we must accept that suffering is a part of life's journey and keep an eternal perspective. When I released all bitterness to the Lord, He was able to restore joy in my heart. What I love about joy is it resides within us all of the time. Happiness differs from joy because it is a fleeting emotion that is triggered by specific moments. Joy, on the other hand, is a long-lasting choice that depends on Jesus, and connects us with meaning and purpose.

The fear of a repeat offense also stole something from me— peace of mind. I know I discussed this more in depth in earlier chapters, but I would like to refer to it once more as I bring this to a close. Peace is when your mind is at ease. Free from worries and anxieties. There are variations of what peace can look like in our lives. Those are spiritual peace, relational peace, psychological peace, and it instills wholeness within us.

It is crucial to understand that peace does not come easily, nor is it guaranteed. While it is a spiritual battle to maintain peace, scripture encourages us that those who are peacemakers are blessed (Matt. 5:9). That said, it is our responsibility to strive for reconciliation with our husband's when choosing to stay. Do this and watch God display His holiness through you and establish peace of mind in your relationship.

> "Strive for peace with everyone, and for the holiness without which no one will see the Lord." (Heb. 12:14, ESV)

The last of these that was robbed from us is hope. When marital betrayal occurs we are apt to become distrusting of our husband's, which is understandable. Distrust and skepticism come easy to humans. That is because it is easier to doubt than to hope and be disappointed again. Yes, the mind battles are discouraging, but God is holy and just. He does not waver and follows through with His promises, unlike mankind.

Maybe today you are in need of repentance for speaking or thinking from a place of doubt about your marriage. If so, this prayer is for you: Lord, forgive me for losing sight of Your ability to restore my marriage. I am sorry for losing hope in the promises You have for me. Thank you for understanding the betrayal, pain, brokenness, and distrust I am going through. Please fill me with hope and strength to believe again in Your ability to redeem my marriage and wait expectantly in hope.

LIVING VICTORIOUSLY

The chains are now released. In this book we identified the spiritual tools God makes available to comfort and guide us, resist the Devil's tactics, forgive daily, and learn the detrimental effects of bitterness. As well as discussed generational curses and how to navigate our way to freedom after battling the rut that infidelity brings. While all of these are helpful to know, they will never complete us if we fail to allow ourselves to be transformed by the power of God. Allowing the Lord to transform you will be an ongoing effort of forgiveness and sanctification that your unbelieving spouse can be sanctified through, deepening your love for each other (1 Cor.

ALLOWING YOURSELF TO BE TRANSFORMED

7:13-14). As you finish this book I hope you leave liberated and that your marriage thrives. May the Gospel of Jesus Christ forever be at the forefront of your mind, guiding you through the Holy Spirit, so that you may defeat the poison of bitterness in unequally yoked marriages. Amen.

About the Author

Kallista Cazares is a nonfiction book editor and copywriter for Christian nonprofit organizations and ministries. She has a BA in English from The University of Texas A&M of San Antonio and lives in South Texas with her husband and three year old daughter. As a born again Christian, Kallista is called to lead her generation to healing and forgiveness. She is passionate about God's Word, her family, lost souls, and hurting marriages. She is adept in how forgiveness can restore hearts and relationships because her lived experiences have allowed her to learn that anything is possible with Jesus.

Kallista offers mentor services, through *Forgive & Stay Christian Coaching*, for betrayed wives who are seeking direction after sexual betrayal. Reservations can be made through Linktree: https://linktr.ee/kallistacazares and you can stay up to date with her on Instagram: @kallistacazares.

Bibliography

Baucham, Voddie. "Love and Marriage: The Better Half." YouTube, January 15, 2013. https://youtu.be/hUvzYcQGZvg?si=BGomopmelR-E5aiO.

Borah, Milt. "Character Is Important for Being a Christian." Argus Leader, November 29, 2019. https://www.argusleader.com/story/news/dell-rapids/2019/11/28/character-important-being-christian/4329925002/#.

Bowden, David. *Rewire your heart: Replace your desire for sin with desire for god.* Nashville, Tennessee: Nelson Books, an imprint of Thomas Nelson, 2018.

Campbell, Aaron. *Love's Expectations* (Soar Book Publishing, 2023), 17.

Enright, In RD, and J. North. "Exploring forgiveness (pp. 46-62)." *Madison: University of* (1992).

"Forgiveness: Your Health Depends on It." Johns Hopkins Medicine, November 1, 2021. https://www.hopkinsmedicine.org/health/wellness-and-prevention/forgiveness-your-health-depends-on-it#:~:tex.

Johnson, Bill. *The Supernatural Power of a Transformed Mind: Access to a Life of Miracles Expanded Edition* (Destiny Image Incorporated, 2016).

Kaplan, Juliana. "The American Nuclear Family Is Officially Over." Business Insider, September 16, 2023. https://www.businessinsider.com/american-marriage-family-structure-kids-over-2023-9?amp.

"Learning How to Forgive: 8 Steps to True Forgiveness," Los Angeles Christian Counseling, September 13, 2023, https://lachristiancounseling.com/articles/learning-how-to-forgive-8-steps-to-true-forgiveness#:~:text=Forgiving%20others%20means%20letting%20go,or%20loss%20we%20have%20suffered.

Lindner, Jannik. "Marriage after Infidelity Statistics," GITNUX, June 23, 2024, https://gitnux.org/marriage-after-infidelity-statistics/.

Maximets, Natalie. "Can a Marriage Survive without Trust: Online Divorce." OnlineDivorce.com, January 29, 2024. https://www.onlinedivorce.com/blog/can-marriage-survive-without-trust/.

BIBLIOGRAPHY

McLanahan, Sara, and Gary D. Sandefur. *Growing up with a single parent: What hurts, what helps.* Cambridge, Massachusetts: Harvard University Press, 1996.

Mróz, Justyna, and Kinga Kaleta. "Forgive, Let Go, and Stay Well! The Relationship between Forgiveness and Physical and Mental Health in Women and Men: The Mediating Role of Self-Consciousness." International journal of environmental research and public health, June 26, 2023. https://www.ncbi.nlm.nih.gov/pmc/articles/PMC10341467/#B5-ijerph-20-06229.

Palmer, Nika. "Self-Love Is a Feminist Issue." Medium, January 23, 2020. https://medium.com/@nikapalmer/self-love-is-a-feminist-issue-7e26e92f0c43.

Ritchie, Jason K. *Oh God Why Can't I Stop: How God's Response to Failure Conquers Shame and Paves Your Way to Victory* (Houston, Texas: Stellar Communications, 2022).

Ryan, Isa. The failing logic of feminism and the "red pill," October 4, 2023. https://substack.com/home/post/p-137657373?utm_campaign=post&utm_medium=web.

"Understanding the Impact of Divorce on Children." Shaheen & Gordon Attorney's at Law, January 31, 2024. https://www.shaheengordon.com/blog/2024/january/understanding-the-impact-of-divorce-on-children/#:~:text=The%20psychological%20effects%20of%20divorce,in%20their%20own%20adult%20olives.

www.ingramcontent.com/pod-product-compliance
Lightning Source LLC
Chambersburg PA
CBHW071211160426
43196CB00011B/2258